BECOMING LIKE JESUS

BIBLE STUDY GUIDE
SIX SESSIONS

THE EVERYDAY JOURNEY TO LIVING A LIFE OF HOLINESS

MATT CHANDLER

Becoming Like Jesus Bible Study Guide

Published by HarperChristian Resources, 3950 Sparks Drive SE, Suite 101, Grand Rapids, MI 49546, USA. HarperChristian Resources is a registered trademark of HarperCollins Christian Publishing, Inc.

Requests for information should be addressed to customercare@harpercollins.com.

ISBN 978-0-310-16527-9 (softcover)
ISBN 978-0-310-16528-6 (ebook)

HarperChristian Resources titles may be purchased in bulk for church, business, fundraising, or ministry use. For information, please email ResourceSpecialist@ChurchSource.com.

Published in association with Yates & Yates (www.yates2.com).

HarperCollins Publishers, Macken House, 39/40 Mayor Street Upper, Dublin 1, D01 C9W8, Ireland (https://www.harpercollins.com).

Art direction: Ron Huizinga
Cover Design: © 2025 HarperCollins Christian Publishing
Interior Design: Inside Out Design

First Printing January 2026

CONTENTS

THE JOURNEY

What does Jesus want from you? Take a moment to think about that question. What does Jesus want from you—really?

The good news is that you don't have to guess. Jesus, quoting from Deuteronomy 6:5, said the greatest commandment is to "Love the Lord your God with all your heart, with all your soul . . . and with all your strength" (Mark 12:30 CSB). You are to love God with your strength, body, and soul. So it's not a biblical stretch to say that what Jesus wants *from* you *is* you.

Jesus isn't interested in just *parts* of you. He wants *all* of you. He wants all your life for all of your life. There is nothing in your past, or any current struggle, or some future failure from which He will distance Himself. He has promised that He will "never leave you nor forsake you" (Hebrews 13:5 ESV) and that He will be "with you always" (Matthew 28:20 CSB).

Furthermore, Jesus wants to use everything you experience to transform you. The Bible paints a reality filled with pain, disappointment, sickness, death, and turmoil. But it also depicts one filled with moments of joy, delight, and gladness. Your journey with Jesus will not always be "up and to the right"—ever increasing in happiness without mingling in the pain and suffering. Rather, Jesus has said what you, as His follower, can expect: "I have told you these things so that in me you may have peace. You will have suffering in this world. Be courageous! I have conquered the world" (John 16:33 CSB). Yes, you will get seasons of Jesus' peace and His victory. But you should also expect the hard seasons.

Jesus presents a picture in Matthew 5:3–10 of what He wants to accomplish in you as you go through these seasons. These verses, called the Beatitudes, describe eight things that He desires to grow in you. Each of these traits is preceded by the word *blessed*, but the Greek word (*makarios*) actually translates to "happy." So, happy are the poor in spirit, those who mourn, the humble, those who hunger and thirst for righteousness, the merciful, the pure in heart, the peacemakers, and those who are persecuted because of righteousness.

Biblical happiness speaks of a joy that *transcends* life's circumstances. This is why the disciples could rejoice after being beaten (Acts 5:41), why Job could worship God after losing everything (Job 1:20–21), and why Jesus could say "those who mourn" are happy (Matthew 5:4). This is what is in view in the Beatitudes—a joy born of knowing and trusting God rather than a subjective feeling. It is also the invitation of this study: to help you see how every high and low in the journey of life is transforming you into the person Jesus wants you to become.

— MATT CHANDLER

HOW TO USE THIS GUIDE

Charles Spurgeon, the renowned English preacher, once said, "The man who is quite satisfied with the name of a Christian, without the life of a Christian, will never see God nor anything at all until his eyes are divinely opened."[1] The Beatitudes are not a checklist for spiritual goals but a portrait of the kind of person Jesus wants you to become. They divinely open your eyes and reveal what it means to be a Christian in more than just name alone.

For this reason, a key point of this study is to have a willingness to do the **deep work** with honesty. There is no other way for transformation to happen. Also, be gentle with yourself. Becoming like Jesus is a journey that happens **over time**, and you are going to notice patterns and lessons that you will have to learn—and probably re-learn. Finally, walk through this adventure with your fellow brothers and sisters in Christ **in community**. God will use them to help you grow.

Before you begin, know that there are a few ways you can go through this material. You can experience this study with others in a group (such as in a Bible study, a Sunday school class, or other type of gathering), or you can go through the content on your own. Either way, the videos are available for viewing at any time by following the instructions provided with this study guide.

GROUP STUDY

Each of the sessions is divided into two parts: (1) a group study section and (2) a personal study section. The group study section provides a basic framework on how to open your time together, get the most out of the video content, and discuss the key ideas that were presented in the teaching. Each session includes the following:

- **Welcome:** A short opening note about the topic of the session for you to read on your own before you meet as a group.

- **Connect:** An icebreaker question to get you and your group members thinking about the topic and interacting with each other *or* a time for the group members to discuss insights from the prior week.
- **Watch:** An outline of the key points covered in each video teaching along with space for you to take notes as you watch each session.
- **Discuss:** Questions to help you and your group reflect on the teaching material presented and apply it to your lives.
- **Respond:** A short personal exercise to help reinforce the key ideas.
- **Close:** A brief set of prompts to help you and your group members take the next step in inviting Jesus to be present and active in your lives.

If you are doing this study in a group, make sure you have your own copy of the study guide so you can write down your thoughts, responses, and reflections in the space provided—and so you have access to the videos via streaming. You will also want to have a copy of the *Becoming Like Jesus* book, as reading it alongside this guide will provide you with deeper insights. (See the notes at the beginning of each group session and personal study section on which chapters of the book you should read before the next group session.)

Finally, keep these points in mind:

- **Facilitation:** If you are doing this study in a group, you will want to appoint someone to serve as a facilitator. This person will be responsible for starting the video and keeping track of time during discussions and activities. If you have been chosen for this role, there are some resources in the back of this guide that can help you lead your group through the study.
- **Faithfulness:** Your group is a place where tremendous growth can happen as you reflect on the Bible, ask questions, and learn what God is doing in other people's lives. For this reason, be fully committed and attend each session so you can build trust and rapport with the other members.
- **Friendship:** The goal of any small group is to be a place where people can share, learn about God, and build friendships. So make your group a safe

place. Be honest about your thoughts and feelings, but also listen carefully to everyone else's thoughts, feelings, and opinions. Keep anything personal that your group members share in confidence so that you can create a community where people can heal, be challenged, and grow spiritually.

If you are going through this study on your own, read the opening Welcome section and reflect on the questions in the Connect section. Watch the video and use the outline provided to help you take notes. Finally, personalize the questions and exercises in the Discuss and Respond sections. Close by recording any requests you want to pray about during the week.

PERSONAL STUDY

The personal study is for you to work through on your own during the week. More than just being a "checklist" for you to complete, this section encourages you to *meditate* on the truths of God's Word, *abide* in Christ (both in the moment and throughout the day), and *join* with others in community (either your small group members or other followers of Jesus). Make it a point to do the three personal studies in each session over the course of three days, as this will help you build a routine of regularly meditating on Scripture and abiding in Christ.

If you are doing this study as part of a group, and you are unable to finish (or even start) these personal studies for the week, you should still attend the group time. Be assured that you are still wanted and welcome even if you don't have your "homework" done. The group studies and personal studies are intended to help you hear what God wants you to hear and apply what He is saying to your life. So, as you go through this study, be listening for Him to speak to you as you discover what it means to truly become like Jesus.

WEEK 1 *at a glance*

THIS WEEK'S READING	Chapters 1–2 in *Becoming Like Jesus*
GROUP MEETING	**Read the Welcome and Connect with the group (page 2)** **Watch the video and take notes (pages 3–4)** **Discuss the questions that follow (page 5)** **Respond to the teaching and Close (page 6)**
PERSONAL STUDIES: STUDY 1 STUDY 2 STUDY 3	 "Spiritual Surrender" (pages 9–12) "Back and Forth" (pages 13–16) "Holy Harmony" (pages 17–20)
JOIN IN COMMUNITY (BEFORE WEEK 2 GROUP MEETING)	**Connect with another believer during the week** **Complete any unfinished studies (page 21)**
NEXT WEEK'S READING	Chapters 3–4 in *Becoming Like Jesus*

SESSION ONE

THE INVITATION:

THE JOURNEY ISN'T LINEAR

Now when Jesus saw the crowds, he went up on a mountainside and sat down. His disciples came to him, and he began to teach them.

MATTHEW 5:1-2

WELCOME | READ ON YOUR OWN

If you are a follower of Jesus, you have certainly been to the *mountaintop* at some point in your life. You've had significant and transformative encounters with God and felt His presence moving. Yet it's also true, if you are a follower of Jesus, that you've spent your fair share of time in the *valley*. Life is both beautiful and brutal, lovely and lonely, carefree and challenging.

Your spiritual journey *will* consist of both highs and lows . . . and that is a good thing. You need the mountaintop highs so you can witness what God is capable of doing—those times you experience the joy that comes from knowing your heavenly Father is lavishing His love on you. But you also need the valley lows—those less joyful times when it feels like you are stuck. Without those valley lows, you can't appreciate the mountaintop highs.

Sure, it would be great to fast-forward through the lows and arrive at the place you want to be. But that is not how spiritual formation works! Becoming like Jesus is a process of making mistakes, humbling yourself, asking forgiveness, being restored, and then learning from your failings. The key is to recognize that *you are moving forward even if you feel stuck*. Jesus cares too much about you to let you waste your time or your experience.

CONNECT | 10 MINUTES

If you or any of your group members don't know each other, take a few minutes to introduce yourselves. Then discuss one or both of the following questions.

- Why did you decide to join this study? What do you hope to learn?

  — or —

- When you think of the Beatitudes, what immediately comes to mind?

WATCH | 25 MINUTES

Watch the video for this session, which you can access through streaming (see the instructions provided with this guide). Below is an outline of the key points covered during the teaching. Record any key concepts that stand out to you.

OUTLINE

I. Spiritual formation is like a horizontal coil with continual highs and lows.

A. You need both life's ups and downs to become a mature believer who is moving forward.

B. The highs are necessary to gain the vantage point of all that God is capable of doing.

C. The lows are needed to experience the grace and love of God when you are at your worst.

II. Spiritual formation takes deep work and must be a priority in your life.

A. Be wary of just "going through the motions" and not truly abiding in Christ.

B. Cultivate a life that delights in spending time with Him through various avenues.

C. Check in with Jesus throughout the day—not just when you need something.

III. Remember that spiritual formation doesn't happen overnight.

A. All of life is a process—you don't arrive at the end until you're at the end.

B. You will stumble forward and learn the same lessons again and again.

C. So be gracious with yourself, and know that you're still moving toward Jesus.

IV. You were not meant to go through the process of spiritual formation alone.

A. God has given your fellow believers to encourage you and to provide you with accountability.

B. You need these fellow believers to help point out your blind spots.

C. You won't grow if you never allow other people to speak life into you or call you out!

NOTES

DISCUSS | 35 MINUTES

Discuss what you just watched by answering the following questions.

1. Ask someone in the group to read aloud Galatians 2:11–21. Peter had previously declared that "God does not show favoritism" (Acts 10:34) and had eaten with the Gentiles. What do you find him doing in this passage—and why? How does Peter's life illustrate the principle that spiritual formation is much like a horizontal coil with highs and lows?

2. Jesus said, "I am the vine, you are the branches. He who abides in Me, and I in him, bears much fruit; for without Me you can do nothing" (John 15:5 NKJV). What does it mean to *abide* in Christ throughout your day? How is this different than just having a set time (like in the morning) where you pray, journal, and read passages from the Bible?

3. Ask someone to read aloud Psalm 1:1–3. What does it mean to meditate on Scripture in the way the psalmist describes? How is this different than just reading the Bible like you would scroll through a news feed—for merely the facts and figures?

4. Now invite someone to read Hebrews 10:24–25. How have your fellow brothers and sisters in Christ encouraged you and spurred you on toward love and good deeds? How have they helped you to see any spiritual "blind spots" in your life?

5. Jesus didn't come to *find* Beatitude people but to *make* them. What is the most daunting aspect of this truth when you consider the traits that Jesus describes in the Beatitudes? How does it encourage you to know that His plan is for you to possess all these traits—and what are you willing to do to lean into the work that He wants to do in you?

RESPOND | 10 MINUTES

The process of becoming like Jesus is like a horizontal coil. You loop through what Jesus describes in the Beatitudes—poverty in spirit, mourning, humility, mercy, and the rest—again and again, but each time at a deeper level. As the apostle Paul writes, this process is not something that happens immediately but something that occurs gradually over time:

> 17 Now the Lord is the Spirit, and where the Spirit of the Lord is, there is
> freedom. 18 And we all, who with unveiled faces contemplate the Lord's glory, are being transformed into his image with ever-increasing glory, which comes from the Lord, who is the Spirit.
>
> **2 CORINTHIANS 3:17–18**

Consider what part of the "coil" you might be in right now when it comes to your spiritual life. Do you feel you are more at the top (the mountaintop) or at the bottom (the valley)? What is happening right now in your life that makes you feel that way?

Now look back on your spiritual journey—whether that is months or decades—and consider some of the ways that Jesus has moved you through the "coil." Are there any lessons He has had you go through again and again? If so, why might He be requiring you to repeat those lessons?

CLOSE | 10 MINUTES

Close by thanking Jesus for giving you a clear path to follow in learning how to become more like Him. Pray that during the course of this study you will choose to abide in Him and remain committed to doing the deep work, over time, in community that is required for you to grow. Pray for patience with yourself and the other members as you all take the next step in discovering how to be the type of Beatitude people whom Jesus wants you to be.

SESSION ONE

PERSONAL STUDY

When you put your faith in Jesus, you were indwelt by the Holy Spirit. Jesus called Him "the Spirit of truth" and said He would "guide you into all the truth" (John 16:13). One of the ways the Holy Spirit does this is by transforming your mind as you *meditate* on the truths of God's Word, *abide* in Christ, and *join* with others in community. This is the goal of these personal studies—not to provide you with a "checklist" to mark each day but to invite you to spend time in God's presence, learn from Him, connect with others, and then wire moments into your day where you're checking in with the Lord. If you are doing this study in a group, be sure to write down your responses to the questions, as you will be given a few minutes to share your insights at the start of the next session. Also, if you are reading *Becoming Like Jesus* alongside this study, you may want to first review the introduction and chapters 1–2 of the book.

"Come to me, all you who are weary and burdened, and I will give you rest."

MATTHEW 11:28

STUDY 1

SPIRITUAL SURRENDER

"Humble yourselves before the Lord, and he will lift you up" (James 4:10). When it comes to what God wants from you . . . it is this. He wants you to surrender every ounce of yourself to Him. This isn't God being an egomaniac. It is God, as a loving Father, wanting you to trust that He knows what is best for you—because no one knows what He knows.

The spiritual life is one of cycles. Sometimes you will, in fact, be on the mountaintop and experience the joy of seeing everything clearly. But inevitably, you will make your way down. Your descent might feel as if you are wandering around and losing your perspective. Or it might feel as if you are plummeting down, hitting every rock and tree until you land face-first in the dirt at the bottom. You go from viewing otherworldly beauty and experiencing inexpressible joy to the hand of God wiping your face and binding your wounds with His grace.

The interesting thing is that this cycle will repeat. You will find yourself struggling with the same things you've battled before, which will feel frustrating and defeating to you—not to mention confusing. But this is where you submit to God. You allow Him to work out the deep roots of your *flesh* so that a deeper root of *faith* can grow. You trust that when you humble yourself before Him—allowing Him to do that painful work—He will lift you up and replace those roots with something that produces beauty in your life.

This is the process of sanctification. With each rise, the beauty becomes more breathtaking and you learn to respond better to the falls. You start to recognize earlier when you are getting off track and are quicker to confess and forgive. You find that you can delight in God's presence. And as you discover how to continually abide in Him, do the deep work that is required, and join in with the other saints, you really do start to become like Jesus.

Meditate on God's Word: 1 Peter 5:6–9; Jeremiah 20:7–13; Romans 8:35–39

1. Your spiritual life can be described as a horizontal coil with constant ups and downs that are moving you in a forward direction. Using the diagram below, mark some of your highs and lows.

2. Read 1 Peter 5:6-9. What does Peter say about surrendering yourself to the Lord? What can you know for certain when you stand firm in the faith?

Jeremiah says that when God called him as a young man, "The LORD reached out his hand, touched my mouth, and told me: I have now filled your mouth with my words. See, I have appointed you today over nations and kingdoms to uproot and tear down, to destroy and demolish, to build and plant" (Jeremiah 1:9–10 CSB). Almost every time Jeremiah says what God wants him to say, he is mocked, beaten up, and one time, thrown into a ditch. In complete frustration, Jeremiah cries out, "You deceived me, LORD, and I was deceived. You seized me and prevailed. I am a laughing-stock all the time; everyone ridicules me" (20:7 CSB). The Hebrew word here (*pathah*) means to entice, seduce, or deceive. Can you imagine someone praying like that in your small group?[2]

3. Jeremiah lived a life of surrender to the Lord—yet faced trials and persecution at almost every turn. What is the nature of his complaint against God in Jeremiah 20:7–8? How does he describe his dilemma in verse 9 if he does *not* speak the Lord's words?

4. What did Jeremiah acknowledge about the Lord in verses 11–12? Given this, do you think he really had any regrets about surrendering himself to God's will? Why or why not?

> Now here's the invitation I want to extend at the very beginning of this study. You don't have to make this journey alone. The One who sits at the center of reality has offered to be with you through every twist and turn, in every high and every low, and to always stick closer than a brother. Jesus, who wants all of you—mind, heart, and soul—wants to be right in the middle of all of it, providing comfort, guidance, and sustaining grace.[3]

5. Read Romans 8:35–39. Paul also lived a surrendered life to God—and also experienced many trials as a result. In spite of this, what did he recognize about God's presence with him? What does this say about God's promise to you when you surrender to His will?

ABIDE IN CHRIST

Spend some time in prayer surrendering your will to Jesus. Ask that He will show you what it means to commit all of yourself to Him—heart, mind, and soul. Look at your schedule for today and plan at least two additional times when you will check in with Him.

Time #1: ______________________________

Time #2: ______________________________

STUDY 2

BACK AND FORTH

A fascinating story is told in Exodus 17:8–16 of the Israelites going into battle against the Amalekites. Moses, the leader of Israel, had a close relationship with God. He told Joshua, his aide, the Lord's battle plan: "Choose some of our men and go out to fight the Amalekites. Tomorrow I will stand on top of the hill with the staff of God in my hands" (verse 9).

The entire story of the battle takes only a few minutes to read, but the battle itself wasn't over in a matter of minutes. No, it took time . . . a *lot* of time. As long as Moses' hands were raised, the Israelites advanced. But when Moses grew tired and his hands lowered, the Israelites suffered setbacks and had to retreat. Back and forth it went, with the Israelites gaining ground and then losing it, fighting the same battle again and again.

The author adds an interesting detail: Moses wasn't alone up on that hill. Aaron, his brother, and Hur, his brother-in-law, were both with him. They watched as Moses obediently followed God's instructions to lift up his staff and witnessed the resulting success of the Israelites in battle. When they saw that Moses was growing weary, they stepped in to hold up his arms so the Israelites would prevail. God honored their efforts, and eventually "Joshua overcame the Amalekite army with the sword" (verse 13).

This narrative speaks directly to your life. God didn't *immediately* give the Israelites the victory. It required Moses' obedience, Aaron and Hur's support, and Joshua's perseverance to carry the day. In the same way, God will ask you to obey Him, look to others for support, and persevere until the battle is won. Sometimes it will feel as if you are retreating more than advancing, but if you are following God, you can be sure the victory *will* be yours.

Meditate on God's Word: 2 Corinthians 4:16–18; Exodus 17:8–16; Hebrews 12:1–3

1. Remember there is nothing so shameful, awful, or wicked you have done that would cause Jesus to distance Himself from you. So, if there is anything in your past weighing you down today, first list those out below, and then actually *give* them over to Christ.

2. Read 2 Corinthians 4:16–18. It can be easy to lose heart when you feel like the battle is going back and forth and you aren't making progress. What assurance does Paul provide that you *are* progressing? What does it mean to focus on things "unseen"?

In March 2022, my son, Reid, asked if I would try Brazilian jiu-jitsu with him. I don't think anything lines up with the kind of journey we're on with Jesus quite like it. Most of us have come to believe that our growth will always be "up and to the right." We can accept that the beginning of any new endeavor might be challenging, but eventually, that will be replaced by an expertise that leads to all joy and no pain. In Brazilian jiu-jitsu, new positions, styles, attacks, and opponents are introduced repeatedly. I'm not saying there aren't fundamentals that matter, but applying those fundamentals must be relearned and reapplied the entire time you train. That's what life is really like.[4]

---

3. Read the full story of the Israelites' battle against the Amalekites in Exodus 17:8–16. Moses, Joshua, and the people had fought battles before, but what "fundamentals" did they have to learn in this situation when it came to trusting and obeying God?

4. What was Joshua's role in this story as Moses, supported by Aaron and Hur, held up the staff of God in his hand? What was required on his part for the Israelites to prevail?

> I've spent a lot of time with Christians who are losing heart or feeling thin in the journey. Part of that is the misunderstanding of progressive sanctification as being up and to the right. If you are judging how you're doing by victories and losses, then joy is nearly impossible. Every stumble, hardship, or failure will make you move away from the beauty of the gospel and the reality that there is nothing that has happened in your past, no present struggle, and no future concern that Jesus wants distance from.[5]

5. Read Hebrews 12:1–3. Joshua had to stay in the fight, and not lose heart, as the battle with the Amalekites went back and forth. What does this passage say about the importance of exhibiting this same kind of perseverance in your spiritual battles?

ABIDE IN CHRIST

Spend time in prayer asking Jesus to help you not lose heart. Express any frustrations you have about your battles and ask Him for the victory. Review your schedule for today and plan at least two additional times when you will check in with Him.

Time #1: ______________________________

Time #2: ______________________________

STUDY 3

HOLY HARMONY

When composers set out to write original scores, they come up with chords—combinations of two or more notes played together—to create melodies, harmonies, and rhythms. They use these chords to develop a main theme that is repeated with slight alterations (called *variations*) throughout the work. What they don't do (unless they are writing for beginners) is craft pieces where only one note is played at a time, up and down the scale, repeated again and again.

This is because music is meant to have an effect on you as the listener. In the beginning, you are presented with a simple theme. But soon, as the piece develops, you recognize other notes and variations being applied to that theme. The music takes you *back* (by reminding you of the main theme) but also moves you *forward* (by providing you with interesting alterations to that theme). The result is a more interesting, engaging, and inspiring piece.

The process of becoming like Jesus is often comprised of familiar and repeating themes. God, the Master Composer, will give you a key theme in your life, and you will find that you are often returning to that theme. However, if you have a discerning ear, you will recognize that each cycle of the theme incorporates a God-given variation. You are not hearing the same thing. God is building on what has come before to move you ahead.

For instance, you will not understand what it means to be meek like Jesus the first time God plays that theme. No, you will need to return to that theme and see the different ways it plays out as God takes you from one movement to the next. As this happens, you will discover that God is moving you *ahead* even as He takes you *back*. And in the end, if you allow the Master Composer to lead you in this way, He will create a holy harmony in your life.

Meditate on God's Word: Philippians 1:9–11; Romans 12:1–2; 1 Thessalonians 5:23–24

1. Think about God being a Master Composer who gives you a "key theme" and asks you to repeat it (with variations). What are some of these key themes in your life? How has God moved you *ahead* even as He has taken you *back* to repeat those themes?

2. Read Philippians 1:9–11. It takes a discerning ear to recognize the work that God is doing in your life. What is Paul's prayer for the Philippian believers in this regard? Why does he want them to have spiritual discernment?

Over time, the Beatitudes begin to reinforce one another in beautiful and unexpected ways. Purity of heart sharpens your hunger for righteousness; meekness teaches you to offer mercy; mourning opens space for peace to be made. Peacemaking, in turn, reveals how far you have yet to go in poverty of spirit. Persecution, when it comes, tests the very fabric of your formation and reveals what's truly rooted. Remember, these are not eight separate qualities but a single tapestry woven together by the Spirit's hand. As the loops in the coil return you again to the same truths, you are not simply relearning—you are being reformed. You are not simply checking boxes on a holiness to-do list but are becoming the kind of person who looks like Jesus in the totality of life.[6]

---

3. Read Romans 12:1–2. The "tapestry" of the Beatitudes represents a pattern moved by the Holy Spirit that is very different from the pattern of the world. What does Paul say about the world's pattern in this passage? Why are you not to conform to it?

4. What does it mean to be transformed by the renewing of your mind? How might God be doing this in your life by having you return to the same truths again and again?

> I once watched a man weep in my office, not because he had committed a fresh sin but because he had finally come to see the roots of an old one. That's sanctification. It's not sinning less and less, though we hope for that; it's seeing sin more clearly and running to Jesus more quickly. It's not about getting stronger but becoming more dependent. It's about trading illusion for reality, over and over again. This is the Spirit's quiet, relentless work: layering mercy upon hunger, meekness upon mourning, purity upon poverty.[7]

5. Read 1 Thessalonians 5:23–24. Sanctification is not sinning less and less but seeing sin more clearly and running to Jesus more quickly. What was Paul certain that God would do in this regard in the lives of the Thessalonian believers? How have you witnessed the Lord's faithfulness when it comes to the way that He is sanctifying you?

ABIDE IN CHRIST

Pray that you will work in harmony with Jesus when it comes to how He is transforming you. Praise Him for the work you have already seen Him accomplish. Take a look at your schedule for today and plan at least two additional times you will check in with Him.

Time #1: ______________________

Time #2: ______________________

JOIN IN COMMUNITY

Remember that one of the goals of this study is to encourage you to check in one-on-one with a fellow brother or sister in Christ. This is because becoming like Jesus happens in community, working alongside others in the journey and not in isolation. So, even if you are not doing this study as part of a small group, make it a point sometime this week to connect with another believer in Christ. Use any of the following prompts to help guide your discussion.

- How have you been abiding in Christ this week? How have you seen this practice begin to transform your relationship with Jesus?
- What steps have you been taking this week to meditate on God's Word? What impact has this had on you thus far?
- What do you find to be the most difficult part of surrendering yourself completely to Christ? Why do you think that is so difficult for you?
- What lessons is God asking you to continually relearn? How has this week's teaching given you some perspective on why He might be doing this?
- What is the most daunting aspect of the Beatitudes for you? How does it encourage you to know Jesus' plan is for you to possess all those traits?

Use this time to go back and complete any of the study and reflection questions from previous days that you weren't able to finish. Make a note below of any revelations you've had and reflect on any growth or personal insights you've gained.

Read chapters 3–4 in *Becoming Like Jesus*. Use the space below to make note of anything in those chapters that stands out to you or encourages you.

WEEK 2 *at a glance*

THIS WEEK'S READING	Chapters 3–4 in *Becoming Like Jesus*
GROUP MEETING	Read the Welcome and Connect with the group (page 24) Watch the video and take notes (pages 25–26) Discuss the questions that follow (page 27) Respond to the teaching and Close (page 28)
PERSONAL STUDIES: STUDY 1 STUDY 2 STUDY 3	 "Asking for Crumbs" (pages 31–34) "Gift of Conviction" (pages 35–38) "Doers of the Word" (pages 39–42)
JOIN IN COMMUNITY (BEFORE WEEK 3 GROUP MEETING)	Connect with another believer during the week Complete any unfinished studies (page 43)
NEXT WEEK'S READING	Chapters 5–6 in *Becoming Like Jesus*

SESSION TWO

POVERTY AND GRIEF:

THE BEAUTIFUL BEGINNING

"Blessed are the poor in spirit, for theirs is the kingdom of heaven. Blessed are those who mourn, for they will be comforted."

MATTHEW 5:3-4

WELCOME | READ ON YOUR OWN

Spiritual maturity, as you discussed last week, is not a process of moving "up and to the right." It is not a set of stairs that you are continually climbing as you move toward sanctification. Rather, growing to be like Christ is more of a horizontal coil where you experience lows (lessons you learn and relearn) and highs (reaching a level of maturity). Jesus has come to make Beatitude people, and that starts not by entering at the top but at the bottom.

The traits that Jesus mentions in the Beatitudes interact with each another. So it is little surprise to find He begins with *poverty of spirit*. This trait opens the door to the work that He wants to do within you. When you truly recognize your utter need for God, all pretenses collapse, self-reliance crumbles, and something honest begins. This is why every true movement toward Christlikeness begins not with strength but with surrender.

The act of being poor in spirit then leads to a godly grief over sin. You *mourn* your sin and the sin-sick world in which you live. This conviction comes from the Holy Spirit, and He brings you to this place not to make you hang your head in shame but so that you will experience the incredible joy of having a clean and pure heart before the Lord. As you see your own brokenness, you are able to see the brokenness around you. This prepares you for the next traits that Jesus wants you to adopt as you move through the Beatitudes.

CONNECT | 10 MINUTES

If you or any of your group members don't know each other, take a few minutes to introduce yourselves. Then discuss one or both of the following questions.

- What is something that spoke to you in last week's personal study that you would like to share with the group?

  — *or* —

- How do you define what it means to be poor in spirit? Why is it necessary to grasp this trait first in your journey toward spiritual maturity?

WATCH | 25 MINUTES

Now watch the video for this session. Below is an outline of the key points covered during the teaching. Record any key concepts that stand out to you.

OUTLINE

I. You enter into the kingdom of God from a low position.

A. Salvation begins with recognizing your spiritual poverty and dire need.
B. You surrender your self-reliance and embrace your dependence on God.
C. The kingdom of God is given to those who come empty-handed and are humble.

II. Poverty in spirit enables you to see the futility of earthly pursuits.

A. Achieving worldly goals doesn't bring lasting fulfillment or purpose.
B. Temporal successes cannot fill the eternal void in your heart.
C. Only God can satisfy the deep longing for meaning and wholeness.

III. Mourning over your sin invites God's comfort, grace, and transformation.

A. Godly grief takes place when you become aware of the sin in your life.
B. Grieving the world's brokenness fuels your dependence on God's redemptive power.
C. Conviction is actually an invitation to experience deeper joy and intimacy with Jesus.

IV. The path to lowliness happens through deep work, done over time, and in community.

A. Deep work: Honest prayers and lament cultivate humility and spiritual growth.
B. Over time: Repeated "losses" teach you to rely on God's strength—and not your own.
C. In community: Fellow believers provide encouragement and accountability.

NOTES

DISCUSS | 35 MINUTES

Discuss what you just watched by answering the following questions.

1. Ask someone to read aloud the first two Beatitudes that Jesus mentions in Matthew 5:3–4. Think back to the time when you surrendered your life to Jesus and accepted His gift of salvation. What were the circumstances that led you to accept His grace? How would you describe the posture of your heart—low or high—when you came to Him?

2. Solomon wrote that God has "set eternity in the human heart" (Ecclesiastes 3:11). In what ways have you experienced this God-sized hole in your heart that nothing in the world can fill? How has God used this void to draw you to Himself?

3. Ask someone to read aloud Luke 18:9–14. How would you describe the difference in the way the Pharisee approached God as compared to the tax collector? Why did Jesus say it was the *tax collector* who went home justified before God?

4. Paul wrote that "godly sorrow brings repentance that leads to salvation and leaves no regret" (2 Corinthians 7:10). What is the connection between mourning your sin and experiencing God's joy and blessing? When you think of mourning in this way, why is it a necessary next step in the process of becoming more like Jesus?

5. Ask someone to read aloud Psalm 139:1–4. The deep work of becoming poor in spirit and mourning your sin begins with honest prayers. How could the words of this psalm from King David serve as a model for how to pray those kinds of honest prayers?

RESPOND | 10 MINUTES

Being *poor in spirit* allows you to see your sinful condition and recognize your need for God. *Mourning* your sin allows you to repent and seek the Lord's forgiveness. As James writes, your community of faith has an important part to play in this as well:

> 13 Is anyone among you in trouble? Let them pray. Is anyone happy? Let
> them sing songs of praise. 14 Is anyone among you sick? Let them call
> the elders of the church to pray over them and anoint them with oil in
> the name of the Lord. 15 And the prayer offered in faith will make the sick
> person well; the Lord will raise them up. If they have sinned, they will be
> forgiven. 16 Therefore confess your sins to each other and pray for each
> other so that you may be healed.
>
> **JAMES 5:13-16**

What does James say about sharing both the highs and lows of your spiritual journey with your fellow believers? What role does humility play in being able to do this?

Forgiveness of sins comes from God, but what part does confessing your sins to others play in healing from sin? How have you witnessed this kind of healing in your life?

CLOSE | 10 MINUTES

Close by asking the Holy Spirit to help you not resist the conviction and deep work that He is doing in your life. Admit as a group that you come before God empty-handed, with nothing to offer, and that your very existence is an act of His grace. Ask the Lord to cause you to be poor in spirit and to mourn your sins whenever you disobey His commands. Finally, pray that you would be willing to lean into each other in community as you continue on in this study.

SESSION TWO

PERSONAL STUDY

The image that Jesus presents of being *poor in spirit* is one of destitution or beggarliness. Jesus says you will be blessed when you approach the living God with empty hands.[8] You won't experience any movement toward becoming like Him if you have a sense of entitlement or are holding on to an inflated opinion of yourself. This is why Jesus calls you to humility, which then leads to you recognizing your true (sinful) condition and your need for God's mercy. Reflect on these ideas this week as you continue to *meditate* on the truths of God's Word, *abide* in Christ, and *join* with others in community. If you are doing this study in a group, continue to write down your responses to the questions, as you will be given a few minutes to share your insights at the start of the next session. Also, if you are reading *Becoming Like Jesus* alongside this study, you may want to first review the introduction and chapters 3–4 of the book.

"He has sent me to proclaim freedom
for the prisoners and recovery of sight
for the blind, to set the oppressed free."

LUKE 4:18

STUDY 1

ASKING FOR CRUMBS

The woman was desperate. "Lord, Son of David, have mercy on me! My daughter is demon-possessed and suffering terribly" (Matthew 15:22). You would think that such a heartfelt plea would move anyone to compassion. But Jesus made no immediate reply to the woman, which evidently prompted the disciples to ask that He send her away.

Matthew reveals that Jesus was in the region of Tyre and Sidon—which was Gentile territory—when this took place, and that the woman was a Canaanite. So she understood what Jesus meant when He replied: "I was sent only to the lost sheep of Israel. . . . It is not right to take the children's bread and toss it to the dogs" (verses 24, 26). Jesus was the Messiah, sent to minister among the Jewish people, in fulfillment of Old Testament prophecy. The message of the kingdom of God was to go *first* to God's chosen people.[9]

The woman was undeterred. "Yes, Lord," she agreed. She acknowledged who Jesus was, calling him "Lord" for the third time, while recognizing who she was not—a member of God's chosen people. In this way, she demonstrated that she was poor in spirit and had no right to request anything from Jesus. But then she went a step further and asked for grace: "Yet even the dogs eat the crumbs that fall from their masters' table" (verse 27 ESV). Jesus immediately recognized the woman's faith, and her daughter was healed at that moment.

We come to Jesus like the Canaanite woman did in this story. We acknowledge that He owes us *nothing* and that anything we receive from Him is a gift. The beautiful thing is that Jesus responds when we humble ourselves in this way! He meets us in our place of need and lifts us up. We find that we truly are blessed when we are poor in spirit—when we recognize that we can't save ourselves—and that we receive the kingdom of heaven.

Meditate on God's Word: Romans 12:3–8; Daniel 4:29–37; Matthew 15:21–28

1. Trying to build your own moral universe by looking inward has shipwrecked many souls on the rocks of pride and self-sufficiency. Where do you see evidence of pride and self-sufficiency in your life? How might God be asking you to surrender those areas to Him?

2. Read Romans 12:3–8. How do Paul's words in this passage give you a working definition of what it looks like to live in the mentality of being poor in spirit?

I constantly meet very smart men and women who lack wisdom. They have PhDs, run businesses, are physically fit, etc., but they lack the wisdom to achieve the "blessed" life that Jesus wants to create in us. Jesus loves and wants to cultivate humility of spirit in us. A great definition of what it means to be "poor in spirit" is "to have a spiritual conviction that we have nothing of our own, nothing but what God bestows upon us, and that we can do nothing good without God's help and grace, thus counting ourselves as nothing, and in all throwing ourselves upon the mercy of God; in brief, as the early church father John Chrysostom explains it, "spiritual poverty is humility."[10]

3. Read Daniel 4:29–37. King Nebuchadnezzar II was a brilliant military strategist who was renowned for his impressive building projects. However, what does this story reveal about his lack of wisdom? How did the Lord teach him a lesson in humility?

4. What was Nebuchadnezzar's realization about himself and God at the end of this ordeal? What did the king conclude about those who walk in pride?

The kingdom of God is perhaps the central theme in the New Testament. It occurs fourteen times in Mark, twenty-two in Luke, twice in John, six in Acts, eight in Paul's epistles, and once in Revelation.[11] Put simply, "the Kingdom of God is not merely a realm or place but the rank, rule, reign, dominion, and royal authority of God."[12] This is what the poor in spirit get! The kingdom of God. They get the reign and rule of God over their lives. They also become conduits and ambassadors of that kingdom.[13]

5. Read the full story of Jesus and the Canaanite woman in Matthew 15:21–28. How did the woman's act of being poor in spirit lead to kingdom-of-God blessings in her life? How do you think she became an "ambassador" of what God had done for her?

ABIDE IN CHRIST

Ask Jesus today to show you what it means to come to Him poor in spirit. Thank Him for the kingdom blessings you receive when you approach Him this way. Review your schedule for today and plan at least two additional times when you will check in with Him.

Time #1: ______________________

Time #2: ______________________

STUDY 2

GIFT OF CONVICTION

Jesus' parable of the two sons told in Luke 15:11–32 is a case study in what happens when you are *not* poor in spirit. The story begins when the younger son asks his father for his share of the inheritance. His father complies, and the younger son quickly squanders it in "wild living" (verse 13). When the money runs out, he is forced to eat pig food in order to survive.

Jesus tells us the son at this point "came to his senses" (verse 17). He realized that he was in a state worse than his father's servants. So he decided to return home, humble himself, and ask if his father would hire him. The younger son, in other words, decided to approach his father with a poverty of spirit, and his next statement—that he had "sinned against heaven" (verse 21)—reveals that he was mourning the fact he had rebelled in the first place.

This is what the Holy Spirit will do in your life when you sin. He will *convict* you as a way of getting you back on the straight and narrow road. This is an act of kindness on His part! As you see in Jesus' parable, when the young man humbled himself and repented of his rebellious ways, the father responded with grace. He had a robe put on his son's shoulders, a ring on his finger, and sandals on his feet. He restored the young man to his family.

This gives meaning to Jesus' statement that "blessed are those who mourn, for they will be comforted" (Matthew 5:4). When you, like the prodigal son, come before your heavenly Father poor in spirit and repent of your sins, you will receive the comfort of knowing you are forgiven. You will rest in the assurance that He has restored your relationship—and that He considers you His beloved child. You will be able to move forward without shame!

Meditate on God's Word: 2 Corinthians 7:8–12; Luke 15:11–32; 2 Corinthians 1:3–4

1. Oswald Chambers wrote that "the old Puritans used to pray for 'the gift of tears.'"[14] As you begin this week's personal study, ask God to give you "the gift of tears" over either your own sin or the brokenness that you see in the world. Write down what He reveals to you.

2. Read 2 Corinthians 7:8–12. The apostle Paul had written a "severe" letter to this group of Christians that had led to their repentance. How does Paul describe what it means to have godly sorrow? What had this produced in the Corinthian believers' lives?

> The world presents us with appealing promises—success, power, security, pleasure—wrapped in a beautiful package. It tells us that we will find fulfillment and happiness if we embrace its ways. But what looks like victory is often a trap. The values of the world promise life but bring destruction when we trust in them instead of God.[15]

3. Read the full parable that Jesus told of the two sons in Luke 15:11–32. What appealing promises of the world did the younger son choose to pursue? Where did following after these things lead him—and what steps did he take when he realized he was in that place?

4. What was the older son's reaction when his father welcomed home his prodigal brother and restored him? What was the condition of his heart as compared to his brother?

Jesus isn't being flippant when He says, "Blessed are those who mourn, for they will be comforted" (Matthew 5:4). He isn't asking for some spirit to sprinkle happiness amid heartbreak. This Beatitude permits us to grieve. Comfort is not found by insulating your heart and burying your sadness. Doing so leads to anger and other coping mechanisms. The verse can be translated to read, "Blessed are those who are in a state of mourning." We are blessed to be in a state of mourning when we grieve our own sin, lament the brokenness of the world, and develop the heart of Jesus.[16]

5. Read 2 Corinthians 1:3–4. What should you do when you receive comfort from the Lord? How would this help you to develop the heart of Jesus?

ABIDE IN CHRIST

Spend some time in prayer thanking Jesus for the gift of conviction and godly sorrow. Confess any unconfessed sins that you have to Him today. Review your schedule for today and plan at least two additional times when you will check in with Him.

Time #1: ____________________

Time #2: ____________________

STUDY 3

DOERS OF THE WORD

"But be doers of the word, and not hearers only, deceiving yourselves" (James 1:22 ESV). It's critically important to be poor in spirit and mourn the fact that you've sinned. However, as James states, merely being *aware* that you have fallen short is not enough. You also have to do the deep work—over time and in community—of first confessing your sins and then repenting of them by choosing to go in the opposite direction of your rebellious ways.

How is this done? Well, a good first step is to pray honest prayers. Your heavenly Father already knows what you have done, but something significant happens in *you* when you lament your sins, acknowledge them to God, and ask Him to forgive you. "When I kept silent, my bones wasted away through my groaning all day long" (Psalm 32:3). At a soul level, you take the first step toward healing when you honestly and openly confess your sins to God.

Next, remember that the deep work of progressing in your spirituality takes place over time. You may find that patterns have developed—perhaps ones you are not even aware of—that need to be broken. You may make the same mistakes again and have to confess again. Just realize that you are on a journey with Jesus and give yourself grace. Lean into what God is doing in your life and agree with Him that you are making progress.

Also, don't close out your community. Nothing good comes from isolation. In fact, that is what the enemy wants. He loves to push you into the dark and make you think you're alone. He wants to keep you in a cycle of guilt and shame. You need other believers to help you step back *into* the light and keep you accountable to remain in *the* light. The fact that you are not alone is a priceless gift from God and will aid you greatly in your quest to become more like Jesus.

Meditate on God's Word: Psalm 13:1–6; Ephesians 4:17–24; Romans 12:15–16

1. As you conclude this week's study, is the Holy Spirit convicting you of being a "hearer only" rather than a "doer" of God's Word? If the answer is yes, list some of the ways you can be a "doer" instead of just a "hearer."

2. One of the ways to learn how to pray honest prayers is to read the psalms of lament. Practice today by reading Psalm 13:1–6. What honest feelings does David express to God? What would it look like for you to pray to the Lord in this way?

> Sin distorts by misrepresenting reality, leading people to embrace falsehoods as truth. It's like a fun house mirror. People see themselves, but the reflection is warped—stretched, compressed, or distorted. The image is still recognizable, but it's not accurate. The danger? When someone looks at the distortion long enough, they start to believe it's real. Sin doesn't erase truth; it bends it just enough that we begin to believe a lie. It distorts a right view of God.[17]

3. Read Ephesians 4:17–24. How does Paul describe the way in which sin can darken a person's understanding? What is the result when people are deceived in this way?

4. What does Paul say the Ephesian believers were taught about how they should live? What does it mean to put off the "old self"—and what is involved in doing so?

When Lauren and I visited our good friend Candy, she had been sent home with hospice care, as her cancer had reached the stage where there was nothing else they could do. For two hours we laughed, cried, and prayed together. It was sacred ground. This is where we lean in and mourn. At any given moment, men and women are enduring heartbreak in our families of faith. Our presence and tears go a long way in giving them peace. You don't have to come with a thin platitude or any answers, just your own sadness for them and the hope of Jesus' ultimate victory over disease and death.[18]

5. Read Romans 12:15–16. You need other believers in Christ to help you stay on the path of righteousness. But what else does having a healthy Christian community bring to you? When has someone comforted or celebrated with you in the way Paul describes?

ABIDE IN CHRIST

Claim the promise that Jesus has given you weapons with "divine power to demolish strongholds" (2 Corinthians 10:4). Spend some time contemplating what that means and declaring that you will walk in the victory that Christ has given you. Review your schedule for today and plan at least two additional times when you will check in with Him.

Time #1: ______________________

Time #2: ______________________

JOIN IN COMMUNITY

Connect with another Christ-follower this week to discuss some of the key insights from this session. Use any of the following prompts to help guide your discussion.

- What initially led you to accept Christ as your Savior? How would you describe the posture of your heart when you came to Him?
- "Godly sorrow brings repentance . . . and leaves no regret" (2 Corinthians 7:10). How has this proven to be true in your experience?
- How has being poor in spirit led to kingdom blessings in your life?
- How have you personally witnessed the power of the Holy Spirit's conviction? How has this been a gift and blessing for you?
- Did the Holy Spirit convict you of being a "hearer only" of God's Word? If so, what steps is He prompting you to take to change this?

Use this time to go back and complete any of the study and reflection questions from previous days that you weren't able to finish. Make a note below of any revelations you've had and reflect on any growth or personal insights you've gained.

Read chapters 5–6 in *Becoming Like Jesus*. Use the space below to make note of anything in those chapters that stands out to you or encourages you.

WEEK 3 *at a glance*

THIS WEEK'S READING	Chapters 5–6 in *Becoming Like Jesus*
GROUP MEETING	**Read the Welcome and Connect with the group (page 46)** **Watch the video and take notes (pages 47–48)** **Discuss the questions that follow (page 49)** **Respond to the teaching and Close (page 50)**
PERSONAL STUDIES: STUDY 1 STUDY 2 STUDY 3	 "Small but Mighty" (pages 53–56) "Spiritual Diet" (pages 57–60) "God Alone" (pages 61–64)
JOIN IN COMMUNITY (BEFORE WEEK 4 GROUP MEETING)	**Connect with another believer during the week** **Complete any unfinished studies (page 65)**
NEXT WEEK'S READING	Chapters 7–8 in *Becoming Like Jesus*

SESSION THREE

QUIET STRENGTH AND HOLY HUNGER

"Blessed are the meek, for they will inherit the earth. Blessed are those who hunger and thirst for righteousness, for they will be filled."

MATTHEW 5:5-6

WELCOME | READ ON YOUR OWN

The word *meekness* is typically translated in our culture as *weakness*. If someone were to describe a person to you who is meek, you would likely hear adjectives such as *timid*, *reserved*, *passive*, and even *cowardly*. However, meekness is not weakness or staying quiet or being a doormat—it is strength under control. In the Bible, both Moses and Jesus are called meek, and those men were fierce, spoke the truth, and were not afraid to confront foolishness and sin.[19]

The act of being poor in spirit is the posture you take before God when you recognize your dependence on Him. However, meekness is how you carry yourself toward others. When Jesus states the meek "will inherit the earth" (Matthew 5:5), He is saying that God uses those who have this quality of strength under control to establish order. In the face of the darkness of this world, they are the light of Christ who show others there is a better way.

When you adopt a mindset of meekness, you desire to be in a right relationship with God, others, creation, and yourself. In the words of Jesus, you "hunger and thirst for righteousness," and the promise is that you "will be filled" (verse 6). God draws you into desperation for Himself and then gives you beyond what you knew you needed. You are transformed into a satisfied person—a gentle force to be reckoned with.

CONNECT | 10 MINUTES

Get this session started by discussing one of these questions:

- What is something that spoke to you in last week's personal study that you would like to share with the group?

  — *or* —

- What tends to be your frame of mind when you are ravenously hungry? When is a time recently that you've been in that state?

WATCH | 25 MINUTES

Now watch the video for this session. Below is an outline of the key points covered during the teaching. Record any key concepts that stand out to you.

OUTLINE

I. Meekness isn't being a doormat, staying quiet, or cowering under pressure.

A. Meekness is not weakness but strength and courage under control.

B. Jesus and Moses were meek and not afraid to confront foolishness and sin.

C. True meekness brings joy and blessing through submission to God's will.

II. Trusting the Lord and doing good is central to meekness.

A. Meekness involves trusting God and living out His truth in your daily life.

B. Bringing truth, beauty, and goodness into every sphere reflects God's kingdom.

C. You actively demonstrate your faith through your good works.

III. Those who are meek delight in the Lord and find rest in Him.

A. Meekness is marked by joy and satisfaction in God's presence and power.

B. Resting in God means relying on His strength to accomplish His purposes.

C. Delighting in God aligns your heart with His will and fuels perseverance.

IV. Hungering and thirsting for righteousness leads to true fulfillment.

A. Righteousness means having a right relationship with God, yourself, others, and creation.

B. A desperate hunger for righteousness drives trust, love, obedience, and stewardship.

C. Pursuing righteousness leads to joy, flourishing, and alignment with God's design.

NOTES

DISCUSS | 35 MINUTES

Discuss what you just watched by answering the following questions.

1. Ask someone to read aloud Matthew 5:5–6. What are the qualities of those who are meek, and why does Jesus say they will inherit the earth? What are the qualities of those who hunger and thirst for righteousness, and why does Jesus say they will be filled?

2. Many characters in the Bible demonstrated qualities of meekness, but only two—Moses and Jesus—were actually called meek. How did Moses demonstrate patience and humility as he led God's people? How did Jesus demonstrate humility and complete submission to His heavenly Father's will as He went about fulfilling His mission on earth?

3. Ask someone to read aloud Psalm 37:1–11. These verses reveal what strength under control actually looks like in practice. What two key qualities of being meek are given in verses 3–4? What other two key qualities of being meek are found in verses 7–10?

4. Invite someone else to read aloud Psalm 42:1–4. What language does the psalmist use to describe what it looks like to hunger and thirst for righteousness?

5. Jesus instructs His followers to "seek first the kingdom of God and his righteousness, and all these things [the basic needs of life] will be added to you" (Matthew 6:33 ESV). When you are seeking righteousness, what kinds of "right relationships" are you pursuing? Why do you think Jesus wants you to prioritize seeking righteousness?

RESPOND | 10 MINUTES

When you possess the quality of *meekness*, you trust in the Lord's strength, rest in Him, and wait on Him. You do good and bring God's truth to every situation—a trait that requires you to have a *hunger and thirst for righteousness*. Even more, as David describes in the following passage, you will have a deep affection for God and a longing to be in His presence:

> [1] Keep me safe, my God, for in you I take refuge. [2] I say to the Lord, "You are my Lord; apart from you I have no good thing." [3] I say of the holy people who are in the land, "They are the noble ones in whom is all my delight." [4] Those who run after other gods will suffer more and more. I will not pour out libations of blood to such gods or take up their names on my lips. . . . [11] You make known to me the path of life; you will fill me with joy in your presence, with eternal pleasures at your right hand.
>
> **PSALM 16:1–4, 11**

What stirs your affections for God? How does being in His presence fill you with joy?

What robs you of your affection for God? What lesser loves are you running after?

CLOSE | 10 MINUTES

Close by asking Jesus to give you strength under control so you can proclaim His truth to the world and do the good work that He wants you to do. Praise Him for giving you a hunger and thirst for His righteousness and for shaping you into a Beatitude person. Ask Him to help you to identify any lesser loves you are pursuing so that your whole heart will be set on Him.

SESSION THREE

PERSONAL STUDY

The quality of *meekness* in the Beatitudes should be seen as a "horizontal" trait. While being poor in spirit is the posture you take before God, meekness is the posture you adopt toward others. You don't demand things from them or impose your will on them but instead treat them with gentleness and respect. When you are submissive to God and acting in humility toward others, it creates a desire in you—a *hunger* and a *thirst*—for righteousness. Reflect on these ideas this week as you continue to *meditate* on the truths of God's Word, *abide* in Christ, and *join* with others in community. If you are doing this study in a group, continue to write down your responses to the questions, as you will be given a few minutes to share your insights at the start of the next session. Also, if you are reading *Becoming Like Jesus* alongside this study, you may want to first review the introduction and chapters 5–6 of the book.

"I am the bread of life. Whoever comes to me will never go hungry, and whoever believes in me will never be thirsty."

JOHN 6:35

STUDY 1

SMALL BUT MIGHTY

Shipping on the Mediterranean Sea during the first century AD was dominated by the Roman Empire. Grain from Egypt, timber from Lebanon, copper from Cyprus, textiles from Asia Minor, and fish from Galilee were transported throughout the region. The typical merchant ship of the day was the *navis oneraria*, measuring between one hundred and one hundred sixty feet in length. One of these ships, unearthed during an excavation in 1985, measured one hundred twenty feet and had a rudder that stood only nine feet tall.

James had this type of vessel in mind when he wrote, "Consider ships: Though very large and driven by fierce winds, they are guided by a very small rudder wherever the will of the pilot directs. So too, though the tongue is a small part of the body, it boasts great things" (3:4–5 CSB). The *navis oneraria* was a large and powerful craft, but the direction it traveled was under the control of the pilot. James used this illustration of "strength under control" to speak about the power of the tongue. When you are operating out of meekness, you control your words and steer your life—and especially your relationships—in the right direction.

The commands given in the Bible about how you are to treat others are rooted in the defining characteristics of God. "God is love" (1 John 4:8), and so you are called to "love one another" (John 13:34). God "is merciful," and so you are to "be merciful" (Luke 6:36). Jesus took on the nature of a servant and "humbled himself" (Philippians 2:8), and so you are to "humble [yourself] before the Lord" (James 4:10). When your words and deeds are based in meekness, you are not only doing "to others as you would have them do to you" (Luke 6:31) but also acting in the loving, merciful, and humble way that reflects God's character.

Meditate on God's Word: Ephesians 4:1–2; Philippians 2:5–11; Revelation 20:1–6

1. The culture of today tends to view *assertiveness* as a virtue to embrace and *meekness* as a problem to overcome. What are some of the ways the world tries to discount the quality of meekness? List four specific examples in the circles below.

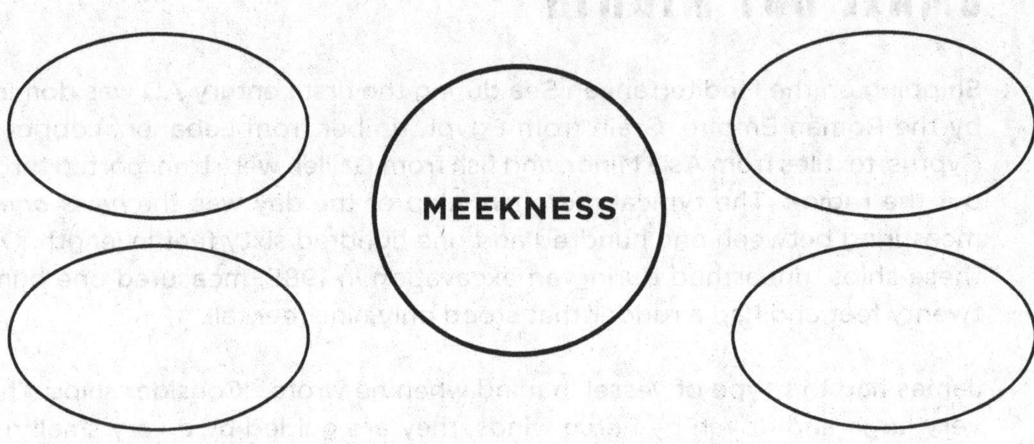

2. Read Ephesians 4:1–2. What did Paul urge the Ephesian believers to do? How would humility lead the way to the other qualities he wanted them to have?

Imagine walking through a house you've lived in your whole life. One day, you open a door you've never noticed before. Inside is a mirror—one that shows you not just how you look but who you are. That's the Bible as a mirror, confronting you with reality, not illusion. But next to that mirror is a map—a map of the future for this house. And it doesn't end with broken rooms and shattered windows; the map shows a full renovation plan: new floors, restored walls, a feast set out in the great room. The Bible doesn't just hold up the mirror and leave you exposed; it hands you the map and says, "This is where I'm taking you. Follow me." Trusting this mirror/map dynamic and our submission to it forms us into the humble men and women who get the blessed life.[20]

3. Read Philippians 2:5–11. Paul provided both a mirror and a map to his churches. He helped people see who they were in Christ and guided them on how to become more like Him. What does Paul say about Jesus' mindset in this passage? What qualities of Jesus does Paul point out that he wanted the Philippian believers to embrace?

4. Think about the church, small group, or Bible study you attend. How can you put these elements of faith into practice in the way you treat others?

Paul, thinking of the future that awaited him with Christ, exclaimed in Romans 8:18, "For I consider that the sufferings of this present time are not worth comparing with the glory that is going to be revealed to us" (CSB). Paul's sufferings were immense. He was tortured, beaten, his friends killed; he was hounded, chased, and imprisoned. The promise of inheriting this new earth with Jesus made all that suffering and hardship seem "light" and "momentary" (2 Corinthians 4:17). It will not be the self-assertive and proud who inherit the earth; it will be those shaped by walking with Jesus in humility who change the world. They and they alone will inherit the earth.[21]

5. Read Revelation 20:1–6. Your future won't be spent strumming a harp in the clouds for eternity. What does this passage reveal is in store for those who desire to become like Jesus? What part does meekness play in attaining this future?

ABIDE IN CHRIST

Ask Jesus to take the helm of your life and steer you to where He wants you to go. Pray for the gift of meekness so you can have a right relationship with others. Review your schedule for today and plan at least two additional times when you will check in with Him.

Time #1: ______________________

Time #2: ______________________

STUDY 2

SPIRITUAL DIET

Jean Anthelme Brillat-Savarin, a French gourmet living in the 1800s, wrote, "Tell me what you eat, and I will tell you what you are."[22] From this came the popular saying, "You are what you eat." The idea is that your physical health, appearance, and even mood can be shaped to some degree by your diet. Science backs up the claim. In one study, researchers at the University of Oxford found that diet can actually affect DNA sequences over generations.[23]

When it comes to your "spiritual diet," what you consume matters as well. You can choose to devote hours of your time to streaming, scrolling, and social media. You can decide to chase after money, or fame, or power, or leisure. You can even focus your life around things that God intends to be good gifts to you, like family, comfort, and success. However, when you fill up your heart and mind with these things—and cling to them as sources of identity, security, and worth—they subtly shift from being gifts and blessings to being false gods.

Chasing after these lesser loves will lead to you feeling unsatisfied and unfulfilled. This is why Jesus instead instructs you to "hunger and thirst for *righteousness*" (Matthew 5:6, emphasis added). When your spiritual diet consists of consuming the truths of God's Word, you become a person who embodies the truths of His Word. You also discover, just as Jesus promised, that you are "blessed" and "filled" (verse 6). Only longings that are centered on Jesus and His righteousness are able to carry the weight of your hope.

And God will replenish you again and again. What He offers, unlike the world, will never run out. Just as you will never arrive at a place where you no longer need sustenance from Him, so He will never come to a place where He is unwilling to provide it for you. As Paul wrote, our God is "able to do far more abundantly than all that we ask or think" (Ephesians 3:20 ESV).

Meditate on God's Word: Philippians 4:8–9; 1 John 3:7–10; Mark 12:28–31

1. Consider what you "consume" on a daily basis when it comes to your time and energy. In what ways are those activities leading you toward God? In what ways might they be subtly leading you away from God? Explain your response.

2. Read Philippians 4:8–9. What "diet" does Paul recommend when it comes to filling your mind? What are some of the benefits you have personally received when you are able to keep your thoughts fixed on what is right, pure, lovely, and admirable?

> Several years ago, I bought my wife, Lauren, an old upright piano. When she tried to play a chord, the dissonance was unmistakable. The problem wasn't that the piano was broken; it was just out of right relationship with the standard. It was out of tune. When the piano technician came to tune it, he didn't smash the piano or replace the keys. He listened, gently adjusted, string by string, key by key, bringing every note back into harmony with A440—the universal pitch standard. When he was done, the piano hadn't changed its identity. It had become what it was meant to be: rightly related, rightly resonant. That's righteousness. Not legal perfection but restored harmony. Not behavior for behavior's sake but fidelity to the relationships for which we were made: relationships with God, others, creation, and ourselves.[24]

3. Read 1 John 3:7–10. Righteousness isn't an abstract moral quality but right-relatedness to God, others, creation, and yourself. What does John say is true of a person who is righteous? How can you know that you (and others) are living in righteousness?

4. Jesus came to destroy the devil's work—to restore humanity's broken relationship with God the Father. What does John say is true of the person who is born of God? How can you know that you (and others) are truly operating as members of God's family?

Right-relatedness to ourselves, according to Scripture, is neither self-centeredness nor self-loathing—it is seeing ourselves rightly in light of who God is and what He has done. In Mark 12:31, Jesus commands, "Love your neighbor as yourself." That command assumes a healthy, God-given form of self-love—not narcissism or pride, but a deep, settled understanding that we are created in God's image, redeemed by Christ, and indwelt by the Spirit. You can't rightly love others if you despise yourself, nor can you walk in righteousness if your identity is built on shame, performance, or comparison. Right-relatedness to ourselves begins with believing what God says about us and treating ourselves accordingly, with humility, grace, and truth.[25]

5. Read Mark 12:28–31. How does the quality of *being poor in spirit* enable you to be right-related toward yourself? How does *meekness* then enable you to be right-related toward others?

ABIDE IN CHRIST

Pray for Jesus to reveal any areas in your life where you are pursuing lesser loves. Ask for His help in reprioritizing your time so you can pursue righteousness. Look at your schedule and plan at least two additional times when you will check in with Him today.

Time #1: ______________________________

Time #2: ______________________________

STUDY 3

GOD ALONE

The young man had the best of intentions. His question to Jesus was sincere: "Teacher, what good thing must I do to get eternal life?" (Matthew 19:16). Jesus answered by telling the man what he already knew: "If you want to enter life, keep the commandments" (verse 17). The man proceeded to ask which ones, prompting Jesus to name off a few. The young man's next statement is telling: "All these I have kept . . . what do I still lack?" (verse 20).

In Luke's account of the story, the man says, "All of these [God's commandments] I have kept since I was a boy" (18:21). He was a faithful follower of God who was doing his best to follow the laws the Lord had established for His people. Yet still . . . he knew that he was *lacking* in something. Luke adds the detail that the young man was not only wealthy but also "a certain ruler" (verse 18). He had money and, at least to some degree, worldly power.

Jesus' answer went to the heart of the man's problem: "You still lack one thing. Sell everything you have and give to the poor, and you will have treasure in heaven. Then come, follow me" (verse 22). When the young man heard this, "he went away sad, because he had great wealth" (Matthew 19:22). Jesus understood the man was serving idols—power, prestige, and wealth. In another teaching, He said "no one can serve two masters" (6:24). The man was trying to serve God *and* his own interests. Jesus was letting him know this wasn't how it worked when it came to God's kingdom. His heart had to be set on serving God alone.

Jesus' invitation is always, "Come, follow me" (Luke 18:22). But He won't allow us to have divided loyalties. His instruction is to "seek *first* [God's] kingdom and his righteousness" (Matthew 6:33, emphasis added). We have to get the order straight if we want to receive all the blessings that Jesus offers to us in the Beatitudes.

Meditate on God's Word: Ecclesiastes 3:9-11; Mark 10:17-31; Philippians 3:10-14

1. The type of hunger that Jesus describes in Matthew 5:6 is the same kind of hunger He experienced after fasting for forty days in the wilderness. Can you say this is the kind of spiritual hunger you feel for pursuing God's righteousness? Why or why not?

2. Read Ecclesiastes 3:9–11. What do you think it means that God has set eternity in the human heart? What does this reveal about our spiritual longings?

> In Hebrews 12:1, we are commanded, "Therefore, since we also have such a large cloud of witnesses surrounding us, let us lay aside every hindrance and sin that so easily ensnares us. Let us run with endurance the race that lies before us" (CSB). The writer makes a distinction between hindrance (*onkos*) and sin (*hamartia*). Sin isn't the only thing we have to throw off. Morally neutral lesser loves are in view here. Anything that robs us of affection for Jesus or creates a sense of spiritual satiety must be dealt with.[26]

3. Read the full story of Jesus' interaction with the rich young man in Mark 10:17–31. How did Jesus hold up a "mirror" to the man and reveal to him who he truly was? What "map" did Jesus give for the man to follow—and why do you think he rejected it?

4. How did the disciples react when Jesus said this (evidently impressive) young man would have a hard time entering the kingdom of God? What blessings did Jesus say the disciples would receive for seeking after Him instead of the comforts of the world?

One of the attributes that belongs to God and God alone is His infinitude. This simply means that Jesus is an inexhaustible well. There is no end to His beauty, power, and goodness. That means there is always more of Him to have, to be experienced, to be known. This knowledge creates a weird satisfaction and a hunger that exist simultaneously. I am satisfied and yet I long for more. I have peace and joy, but there is a greater experience of those things available to me, and I long for them. I have them, and I still haven't found what I'm looking for. This kind of hunger doesn't happen in striving but in knowing. We know that there is more. That changes how we pray, live in obedience, and understand the process of becoming like Jesus.[27]

5. Read Philippians 3:10–14. Paul clearly *knew* Christ, and yet here he says that he *wants* to know Christ. How does this describe spiritual hunger? What does Paul say is the "prize" for every person on the journey toward becoming like Jesus?

ABIDE IN CHRIST

Consider today what you would be willing to give up to follow after Christ. Thank the Lord for His offer to follow after Him—and choose to make that your priority. Review your schedule for today and plan at least two additional times when you will check in with Him.

Time #1: ____________________

Time #2: ____________________

JOIN IN COMMUNITY

Connect with another Christ-follower this week to discuss some of the key insights from this session. Use any of the following prompts to help guide your discussion.

- How would you now describe the qualities of a person who is meek? How did Jesus demonstrate that He was acting in meekness?
- What stirs your affections for being in God's presence? What are some of the lesser loves that rob you of your affection for God?
- How has the Bible served as both a mirror and a map for you? How easy or difficult is it for you to embrace what it reveals to you?
- What are some of the benefits you've received by keeping your thoughts fixed on what is right, pure, lovely, and admirable?
- What stood out to you the most about spiritual hunger and thirst? How has seeking after Christ satisfied you while also keeping you longing for more?

Use this time to go back and complete any of the study and reflection questions from previous days that you weren't able to finish. Make a note below of any revelations you've had and reflect on any growth or personal insights you've gained.

Read chapters 7-8 in *Becoming Like Jesus*. Use the space below to make note of anything in those chapters that stands out to you or encourages you.

WEEK 4 *at a glance*

THIS WEEK'S READING	Chapters 7–8 in *Becoming Like Jesus*
GROUP MEETING	Read the Welcome and Connect with the group (page 68) Watch the video and take notes (pages 69–70) Discuss the questions that follow (page 71) Respond to the teaching and Close (page 72)
PERSONAL STUDIES: STUDY 1 STUDY 2 STUDY 3	 "Justice and Mercy" (pages 75–78) "State of the Heart" (pages 79–82) "Beautiful Multiplication" (pages 83–86)
JOIN IN COMMUNITY (BEFORE WEEK 5 GROUP MEETING)	Connect with someone in your group during the week Complete any unfinished studies (page 87)
NEXT WEEK'S READING	Chapter 9 in *Becoming Like Jesus*

SESSION FOUR

MERCY AND PURITY: RECEIVING AND REVEALING

"Blessed are the merciful, for they will be shown mercy. Blessed are the pure in heart, for they will see God."

MATTHEW 5:7-8

WELCOME | READ ON YOUR OWN

You receive a lot from your heavenly Father when you join His family. Mercy, grace, kindness, forgiveness, love, joy, hope, peace . . . to name just a few of the gifts that He provides. The question for you now, as a developing Beatitude person, is what to do with all you've received. Do you just keep all those blessings for yourself? Or is Jesus asking you to do more?

The answer is found in the next two traits that Jesus mentions: *mercy* and *purity*. When you are acting out of mercy, you are doing unto others what Jesus has done for you. You are not just taking in everything from God—receiving, receiving, receiving—but giving out in equal measure. Mercy, in essence, was the hallmark of Jesus' ministry. He was constantly giving of Himself to others. So, when you are merciful, you are being just like Him.

Your awareness of God's mercy, and your act of extending it to others, awakens you to another need in your life—for purity, integrity, and wholeheartedness. Purity helps you to get honest with God. You recognize that you will sin, but that you don't need to hide your sin from the Lord when you do, because He is merciful and will forgive you. He *will* be merciful toward you in the same way that you have been merciful toward others. You no longer have to be ruled by the shame of your past! You can move ahead in becoming more like Jesus.

CONNECT | 10 MINUTES

Get this session started by discussing one of these questions:

- What is something that spoke to you in last week's personal study that you would like to share with the group?

  — *or* —

- Do you have an example of when you received mercy from someone in your life? What did that person do to show you mercy?

WATCH | 25 MINUTES

Now watch the video for this session. Below is an outline of the key points covered during the teaching. Record any key concepts that stand out to you.

OUTLINE

I. Your life in Christ is meant to be one of receiving *and* giving.

A. The Dead Sea is devoid of life because it takes in but never gives out.

B. Mercy must flow outward to prevent spiritual stagnation and lifelessness.

C. Jesus calls for active mercy, not passive reception, for His followers.

II. Jesus' entire ministry was marked by acts of compassion.

A. Jesus offered forgiveness over judgment to the woman caught in adultery (John 8:1–11).

B. Jesus broke cultural norms by extending fellowship to Zacchaeus (Luke 19:1–10).

C. Jesus addressed the deepest wounds of the Samaritan woman at the well (John 4:1–26).

III. Purity begins with receiving God's mercy and coming to Him as you are.

A. God's mercy allows you to approach Him without hiding or performing.

B. Honest prayers bring your struggles and sins into God's presence and begins the process of transformation.

C. Receiving God's mercy replaces fear and anxiety with joy, freedom, and wholeheartedness.

IV. Practical steps will enable you to become merciful and pure in heart.

A. Create space to meditate on the mercy of God that you've received.

B. Sit with the forgiveness of God in your life and notice how that has changed you.

C. Ask yourself if there is someone from whom you are withholding mercy.

NOTES

DISCUSS | 35 MINUTES

Discuss what you just watched by answering the following questions.

1. Ask someone to read aloud Matthew 5:7–8. What does it mean to be merciful, and what does Jesus say you will receive when you live out this quality? What does it mean to be pure in heart, and how does this lead to you being able to "see" God?

2. Ask someone to read aloud John 8:1–11. The Jewish authorities rightly pointed out that the consequence for the woman's sin under the law of Moses was death. What did Jesus say to make them reconsider this stance? What did Jesus say to the woman that was merciful after all her accusers had left the scene?

3. Jesus said, "Give, and it will be given to you. . . . For with the measure you use, it will be measured to you" (Luke 6:38). What measure of mercy have you received from God? What does it look like to pour out that same measure of mercy to others?

4. Ask someone to read aloud James 4:7–9. When you sin, your natural inclination will be to distance yourself from God. What does James say you should do instead? How is coming to God when you sin a step toward living out the Beatitude of being pure in heart?

5. One biblical author wrote, "Let us then approach God's throne of grace with confidence, so that we may receive mercy and find grace to help us in our time of need" (Hebrews 4:16). What does this say about your ability to approach God where you are right now? What is the danger in thinking you have to "clean up" before you come to Him?

RESPOND | 10 MINUTES

Being *pure in heart* allows you to see that you are not perfect when it comes to living up to God's holy standard. This enables you to be *merciful* to others who also miss the mark. You forgive them—even when it is difficult—because you remember the depth to which God has forgiven you. Paul wrote the following on the importance of extending this kind of mercy:

> 12 Therefore, as God's chosen people, holy and dearly loved, clothe your-
> selves with compassion, kindness, humility, gentleness and patience.
> 13 Bear with each other and forgive one another if any of you has a griev-
> ance against someone. Forgive as the Lord forgave you.
>
> **COLOSSIANS 3:12–13**

What does it mean to "clothe" yourself with compassion, kindness, humility, gentleness, and patience? What does ut look like when you are "wearing" these traits?

Who is someone you need to "bear with" today? How does remembering that you are chosen by God, holy and dearly loved, help you to extend mercy to that person?

CLOSE | 10 MINUTES

Close by spending some time just thanking Jesus for His act of mercy in stepping onto this earth so that you could be saved from your sin. Invite the Holy Spirit to prompt you in the week ahead and show you those moments when you need to bear with others and forgive just as the Lord has forgiven you. Pray for boldness to approach the throne of God's grace whenever you fall into sin, with confidence that He will meet you there and restore you.

SESSION FOUR

PERSONAL STUDY

Jesus doesn't give you any wiggle room when it comes to being *merciful* to others. The term He uses in the Beatitudes (*eleēmōn*) actually means "costly compassion."[28] Mercy comes at the cost of your time and resources to help others—and at the cost of giving up your right to get back at anyone who has wronged you. This is where it also helps to be *pure in heart*. When you realize that God is willing to *not* give you what you deserve, you are willing to extend that same mercy to others. Reflect on these ideas this week as you *meditate* on God's Word, *abide* in Christ, and *join* with others in community. If you are doing this study in a group, continue to record your responses to the questions, as you will be given a few minutes to share your insights at the start of the next session. Also, if you are reading *Becoming Like Jesus* alongside this study, you may want to first review the introduction and chapters 7–8 of the book.

"Be merciful, just as your Father is merciful."

LUKE 6:36

STUDY 1

JUSTICE AND MERCY

Jesus was in Capernaum one day when He saw a man named Matthew sitting at his tax collector's booth. "Follow me," He said to him (Matthew 9:9). Matthew got up, followed him, and even invited Jesus to his home. This did not sit well with the Pharisees. They asked Jesus' disciples, "Why does your teacher eat with tax collectors and sinners?" (verse 11).

Jesus responded, "It is not the healthy who need a doctor, but the sick. But go and learn what this means: 'I desire mercy, not sacrifice.' For I have not come to call the righteous, but sinners" (verses 12–13). The statement that Jesus wanted the Pharisees to "learn" was from Hosea 6:6, in which God rebuked the Israelites for focusing on the letter of the law while ignoring the heart behind the law. God desired *mercy* over strict procedural observances.

Justice means getting what you deserve. To the Pharisees, Matthew was a sinner. He was a person to be cast out and scorned—because it was what he deserved. Jesus wasn't interested in evoking justice against Matthew. He was interested in showing Matthew *mercy*—giving him what he didn't deserve. To Jesus, Matthew was a follower . . . a disciple.

Your salvation is based on both. As a sinner, it is in your nature to rebel against God. Your sins separate you from a holy God, so the only just punishment is an eternity spent separated from His holy presence. It is what you deserve. But God, in His mercy, sent Jesus to pay the price for His justice that you couldn't pay. He gave you what you didn't deserve.

Does this mean you keep sinning? By no means. In fact, when you understand the price Jesus paid on your behalf, it compels you to not be flippant with His gift of mercy. His mercy reshapes your heart, which leads to a transformed life.

Meditate on God's Word: Titus 3:3–8; Luke 5:27–32; 1 Peter 3:8–9

1. In what ways do you tend to view people the way the Pharisees saw Matthew? What would it look like to instead view them the way Jesus saw Matthew?

2. Read Titus 3:3–8. How does Paul describe your condition before you accepted Christ as your Savior? Why did God choose to extend mercy to you—a sinner?

> This undeserved welcome is made most clear in the life and ministry of Jesus. Again and again, He invites the wrong people to the table. The tax collectors, the prostitutes, the outcasts, and the unclean. He doesn't just tolerate them; He eats with them, touches them, and blesses them. His mercy wasn't passive; it was embodied in presence and hospitality. Where the religious leaders excluded, Jesus embraced. Where others saw sin, He saw a story worth redeeming. The mercy of God in Christ doesn't shrink back from our failures; it draws near with open arms and says, "Come home."[29]

3. Read the account of Jesus calling Matthew (also known as Levi) to be His disciple in Luke 5:27–32. Tax collectors were seen by the Jewish people as crooked officials who served a pagan government. What did Jesus do in this passage to reveal that He not only *tolerated* Matthew but also wanted to enter into *fellowship* with him?

4. Jesus' willingness to associate with Matthew offended the Pharisees because they held that truly godly people separated themselves from those whose moral or ritual purity might be in question.[30] How did this contrast with Jesus' view? What did Jesus understand (that the Pharisees did not) about who was in need of God's mercy?

Extending mercy requires us to believe that vengeance belongs to the Lord, not to us. It feels unjust because it asks us to absorb part of the cost. Mercy doesn't deny that wrong was done; it simply chooses not to make the offender carry the full weight. That weight has to go somewhere—and often, the one showing mercy bears it in silence, prayer, and aching hope. This is why mercy is not cheap; it's costly and courageous. It mirrors the cross, where Jesus bore what we deserved so we could receive what we didn't. In that way, mercy feels unjust only until we remember how unjust grace was for us.[31]

5. Read 1 Peter 3:8–9. What does Peter say about the cost of showing mercy? What does it look like, at a practical level, to "repay evil with blessing"?

ABIDE IN CHRIST

Praise God today that He chose to show you mercy through the sacrifice of Christ rather than justice. Pray that you will increasingly become a person of grace and mercy. Review your schedule for today and plan at least two additional times to check in with Him.

Time #1: ______________________

Time #2: ______________________

STUDY 2

STATE OF THE HEART

Jeremiah, prophesying God's words to the people of Judah, wrote, "The heart is deceitful above all things, and desperately wicked; who can know it?" (17:9 NKJV). One of the hardest things in life is to be honest with yourself about yourself. But there is something so freeing about admitting your heart *is* deceitful above all things and desperately wicked—and that at times you don't understand why you let your heart lead you to do what you don't want to do.

Paul expressed this dilemma when he wrote, "I have the desire to do what is good, but I cannot carry it out. For I do not do the good I want to do, but the evil I do not want to do—this I keep on doing" (Romans 7:18–19). It's easy to lead a duplicitous life, but that is the last thing God desires. He wants you to operate as a wholehearted being, not someone who operates one way in public but completely differently in private . . . with a closet full of little pet sins that no one has a clue about. The enemy wants to keep you in the dark. But even the idea of purity brings to mind the idea of light, integrity, and honest transparency. Being pure in heart is coming to God completely as you are, with nothing to hide.

Why does God care so much about your heart? Well, in the words of one wise writer, "Above all else, guard your heart, for everything you do flows from it" (Proverbs 4:23). Your heart represents the core of who you are—your deepest thoughts, desires, and motivations. Ultimately, whatever is on the *inside* of you moves to the *outside* of you. If your heart is filled with anger, you will act out in anger. If it is filled with greed, you will act out in greed. But if, on the other hand, your heart is filled with God's mercy, then you will act out in mercy.

If you want to be pure of heart, you have to be honest about what is in your heart. The good news is that this honesty allows God to transform your heart. He helps you do the deep work, over time, in community, that enables you to grow.

Meditate on God's Word: Romans 3:9–12; Matthew 23:1–7, 25–28; Psalm 51:1–12

1. In what ways can you relate to Paul's statement about *wanting* to do good but finding that you cannot? Why is it so important to be honest with God about this struggle?

2. Read Romans 3:9–12. What does Paul say in the passage about your ability to be righteous on your own? What is the "power" you are living under?

> The purity Jesus speaks of in the Beatitudes isn't a call to moral perfection but to a single-hearted devotion. "Blessed are the pure in heart, for they shall see God" (Matthew 5:8 ESV) doesn't bless the externally impressive but the internally undivided. To be pure in heart is to bring our desires, motives, and longings into honest alignment before the face of God.[32]

3. Read Matthew 23:1–7. Jesus told the people to respect the Pharisees' authority and to obey what they said. However, what did Jesus say about following their example? What was Jesus' complaint when it came to how the Pharisees presented themselves?

4. Now read Matthew 23:25–28. Why did Jesus, in this passage, twice call the Pharisees hypocrites? What does Jesus say was the true state of their hearts?

> What does it look like to actually live with an undivided heart? It looks like being quick to confess and slow to justify. It looks like dragging your private self into the presence of God daily, not with scripted prayers or polished intentions but with raw honesty. It looks like offering your impulses, not just your ideals. Your anger, not just your praise; your motives, not just your actions. To be pure in heart is not to be sinless; it is to be fully present before God with nothing hidden.[33]

5. Read Psalm 51:1–12. What does David honestly acknowledge about the state of his heart? How will you make his prayer for a pure heart your own?

ABIDE IN CHRIST

Take some extended time today to be honest with Jesus about your heart. Confess any ways that you have tried to hide your sins from Him. Look at your schedule for the day and plan at least two additional times when you will check in with Him.

Time #1: ______________________

Time #2: ______________________

STUDY 3

BEAUTIFUL MULTIPLICATION

"What is the kingdom of God like? What shall I compare it to? It is like a mustard seed, which a man took and planted in his garden. It grew and became a tree, and the birds perched in its branches" (Luke 13:18–19). This is an interesting comparison. In biblical times, the mustard plant—which grew from a tiny seed—was invasive. It multiplied and spread so aggressively that farmers had to be cautious about how much of it they planted.[34]

The kingdom of God is like that mustard plant. It has a way of multiplying in your heart, reaching into every area of your life as you allow it to grow. Those who embrace the kingdom value of mercy find that as they give it out . . . they receive it back in return. Mercy has a beautiful way of multiplying. When you spread the seeds of mercy, even though those seeds might be small, they result in an abundant harvest for God's kingdom.

Purity of heart, another kingdom value, is born when you receive the mercy of God. It sharpens your spiritual vision. When you are honest with God, you begin to see Him more clearly—in His Word, in His people, and even in pain—and want to see even *more* of Him. As you allow the seeds of purity to take root in your heart, even though those seeds might be small, they result in an abundant harvest. God purifies not just your behaviors but also your loves, redirecting your affections so you want what He wants.

Paul, speaking of eternity, wrote, "For now we see only a reflection as in a mirror; then we shall see face to face" (1 Corinthians 13:12). The staggering promise of the Christian life is that one day you will see God with your own eyes. In the meantime, keep confessing, keep surrendering, keep forgiving, and keep pursuing a heart of mercy and purity.

Meditate on God's Word: Mark 4:14–20; Luke 7:36–47; Galatians 5:16–18

1. What are some of the ways you've experienced the multiplying effect of mercy? How has spending time in God's presence created a desire in you to know Him more?

2. Read Mark 4:14–20. The "seed" in this story represents the word of God—the gospel. What happens to those who hear the word and accept it?

> Jesus is not teaching us to earn God's mercy by showing it. That would contradict the very nature of mercy. No, He is saying something more profound: that those who have received mercy will become merciful. And in doing so, they will experience that mercy more deeply. Mercy flows from mercy. It is a cycle, not a transaction, like breathing in and breathing out. The more we extend it, the more we understand it. The more we forgive, the more we taste the freedom we have been given. The more we enter someone else's pain, the more we discover Jesus entering ours. Mercy multiplies.[35]

3. Read Luke 7:36–47. What complaint did Simon (the Pharisee) make in his thoughts? What was the point of the story that Jesus told in response?

4. What did the woman do that Simon was unwilling to do? What did Jesus say about how mercy multiplies in the lives of those who have received great mercy from God?

> We do not drift into purity; we're drawn into it by the Spirit, through the Word, in the context of community. We are drawn by a vision of the One who loved us while we were yet sinners and who is faithful to finish what He started. The more our hearts are made whole, the more they long to behold Him. Not His gifts. Not His blessings. But Him. The pure in heart are not morally superior but increasingly undivided in their desire. Jesus' promise, "they shall see God," is future glory, but it also spills into the present.[36]

5. Read Galatians 5:16-18. How have you sensed the Holy Spirit drawing you into purity this week as you've meditated on God's Word? How has He been helping you to have an *undivided* heart—so that you are the same on the inside as on the outside?

ABIDE IN CHRIST

Ask Jesus to help you extend the same degree of mercy to others that He has shown to you. Also pray that the Holy Spirit will continue to lead you into purity. Review today's schedule and plan at least two additional times to check in with the Lord.

Time #1: ______________________________

Time #2: ______________________________

JOIN IN COMMUNITY

Connect with another Christ-follower this week to discuss some of the key insights from this session. Use any of the following prompts to help guide your discussion.

- How difficult is it for you to not seek vengeance against others? How has Jesus been helping you this week to be a person of mercy?
- Jesus was willing to associate with all kinds of people during His ministry. How has He been challenging you to *love* rather than *judge* others?
- What has God revealed to you in this session about the state of your heart? What has been the result of you being honest with Him about it?
- What is the connection between having an awareness of God's abundance toward you and your willingness to extend abundant mercy to others?
- What further steps do you need to take to practice vulnerability in your community? What will you do to start practicing this right now?

Use this time to go back and complete any of the study and reflection questions from previous days that you weren't able to finish. Make a note below of any revelations you've had and reflect on any growth or personal insights you've gained.

Read chapter 9 in *Becoming Like Jesus*. Use the space below to make note of anything in those chapters that stands out to you or encourages you.

WEEK 5 *at a glance*

THIS WEEK'S READING	Chapter 9 in *Becoming Like Jesus*
GROUP MEETING	**Read the Welcome and Connect with the group (page 90)** **Watch the video and take notes (pages 91–92)** **Discuss the questions that follow (page 93)** **Respond to the teaching and Close (page 94)**
PERSONAL STUDIES: STUDY 1 STUDY 2 STUDY 3	 "Into the Chaos" (pages 97–100) "Spiritual Battlegrounds" (pages 101–104) "Willing to Act" (pages 105–108)
JOIN IN COMMUNITY (BEFORE WEEK 6 GROUP MEETING)	**Connect with someone in your group during the week** **Complete any unfinished studies (page 109)**
NEXT WEEK'S READING	Chapters 10–11 in *Becoming Like Jesus*

SESSION FIVE

THE PEACEMAKERS: CARRIERS OF SHALOM

"Blessed are the peacemakers, for they will be called children of God."

MATTHEW 5:9

WELCOME | READ ON YOUR OWN

Conflict is something that seems to be everywhere. You hear about conflicts raging around the world. You witness conflicts in cities and neighborhoods. You get a front-row seat to conflicts that break out at your workplace, church, and home. Tensions always feel as if they are running high, and there appears to be no getting away from it. So what do you do?

You look to the example of Jesus. He was no stranger to conflict. The Jewish religious leaders often challenged Him on His teachings and actions. Many of His followers found His teachings too hard to accept and "turned back" (John 6:66). His own family thought that He was "out of his mind" (Mark 3:21). His disciples argued among themselves "as to which of them would be the greatest" (Luke 9:46). Peter took Jesus aside "and began to rebuke him" (Matthew 16:22) and Judas plotted "how he might betray Jesus" (Luke 22:4).

Jesus understood His message would cause division. But He also knew He was the Son of God who had been sent on a mission—to restore the peace between humans and God. As John wrote, "Yet to all who did receive him . . . he gave the right to become children of God" (John 1:12). Jesus brings the peace of God to those who receive Him. This enables them to be His *ambassadors of peace* and to enter into conflicts with the knowledge of who they are in Him.

CONNECT | 10 MINUTES

Get this session started by discussing one of these questions:

- What is something that spoke to you in last week's personal study that you would like to share with the group?

  — *or* —

- What are some of the triggers—things other people say or do that set you off—that most often lead you into conflicts?

WATCH | 25 MINUTES

Now watch the video for this session. Below is an outline of the key points covered during the teaching. Record any key concepts that stand out to you.

OUTLINE

I. **Jesus instructs you to bring God's kingdom peace into conflicts and chaos.**
   A. Peacemaking is active, not passive, and requires intentional engagement in conflict.
   B. God's peace restores harmony and reflects the wholeness of creation (Genesis 1–2).
   C. True peace is rooted in the gospel—Jesus reconciles you to God and others.

II. **Sin disrupts peace by fracturing relationships with God, self, others, and creation.**
   A. Sin separates you from God, who is the source of your meaning and purpose.
   B. This disconnection leads to not knowing who you are and to you competing with others.
   C. Comparison and competition with others create external chaos and conflict.

III. **Peacemaking requires knowing who you are in Christ.**
   A. Knowing that you are a beloved child of God provides confidence in conflict.
   B. Your identity in Christ frees you from seeking validation through possessions or status.
   C. Your spiritual and natural gifts equip you to serve God and others in peacemaking.

IV. **The act of peacemaking is a process that requires deep work, over time, and in community.**
   A. Honest prayers help you process emotions like anger and fear before engaging in conflict.
   B. Healing relationships often require follow-up and ongoing reconciliation efforts.
   C. Committing to a community fosters growth, accountability, and lasting peace.

NOTES

DISCUSS | 35 MINUTES

Discuss what you just watched by answering the following questions.

1. Ask someone in the group to read aloud Matthew 5:9. How do you describe what it means to be a peacemaker—and how is that different from being a peacekeeper? When is a time that you experienced the joy of being able to resolve a conflict between people?

2. Ask someone to read Genesis 2:1–9. How do you see God's *shalom*—His desire for wholeness and harmony—presented in this account of creation? What does this tell you about His kingdom and the kind of peace He wants you to have?

3. The prophet Isaiah said to the Israelites, who throughout their history had repeatedly fallen into sin, "Your iniquities have made a separation between you and your God" (59:2 ESV). How does sin separate you from God? How does this separation fracture the way you see yourself—giving you a false image of who you are in God's sight?

4. Ask someone to read aloud Ephesians 2:6–10. What does Paul reveal about your true identity in this passage? In your own life, how have you seen comparison and competition rise up within you when you neglect this truth from God's Word?

5. As a follower of Jesus who is becoming like Him, you are called to bring peace to your relationships. Which strategies from the teaching will you put into practice this week to defuse conflict? Why do you believe those strategies would be especially helpful?

RESPOND | 10 MINUTES

Part of becoming a *peacemaker* is learning how to be at peace with yourself—to see yourself as God sees you and align yourself to His will. James, in his letter to the church, pointed out how this kind of spiritual misalignment can lead to all kinds of trouble among believers:

> [1] What causes fights and quarrels among you? Don't they come from your
> desires that battle within you? [2] You desire but do not have, so you kill.
> You covet but you cannot get what you want, so you quarrel and fight.
> You do not have because you do not ask God. [3] When you ask, you do not
> receive, because you ask with wrong motives, that you may spend what
> you get on your pleasures.
>
> **JAMES 4:1-3**

How do you respond to this description of what causes fights and quarrels? How do your own desires play a part in the conflicts that arise around you?

If you are harboring resentment or are in conflict with another person right now, what is the story you are telling yourself? What will you do to check that out with the other person?

CLOSE | 10 MINUTES

Close your time together by asking Jesus to help you fulfill His calling to become a peacemaker in your world. Pray for the Holy Spirit to give you patience and wisdom so you can step back from a heated situation and ask if the story you are telling yourself is true. Ask God to continually remind you of who you are in Christ so you can also see yourself accurately.

SESSION FIVE

PERSONAL STUDY

The picture that Jesus paints of a *peacemaker* is one who enters into a conflict. The peacemaker does not stand on the sidelines or retreat into cowardly silence but wades into the fray with courage, hope, and a mission from God of restoring peace. The peacemaker seeks to stand between those who are fighting and mend what has been torn . . . even at the cost of suffering some collateral damage in the exchange. It is a Beatitude with scars. So reflect on what it really means to be a peacemaker this week as you *meditate* on the truths of God's Word, *abide* in Christ, and *join* with others in community. If you are doing this study in a group, continue to write down your responses to the questions, as you will be given a few minutes to share your insights at the start of the next session. Also, if you are reading *Becoming Like Jesus* alongside this study, you may want to first review the introduction and chapter 9 of the book.

"Peace I leave with you;
my peace I give you. I do not
give to you as the world gives."

JOHN 14:27

STUDY 1

INTO THE CHAOS

"Now the earth was formless and empty, darkness was over the surface of the deep, and the Spirit of God was hovering over the waters" (Genesis 1:2). Into this empty void, the Bible reveals, God spoke and created order. He entered into the chaos to bring His *shalom*—wholeness, harmony, peace—and declared "it was very good" (verse 31).

Jesus likewise stepped into the world to bring God's *shalom*. There are two scenes in the Gospels that especially stand out. In the first, Jesus and the disciples are crossing the Sea of Galilee when a ferocious squall comes up that threatens to sink the boat. The disciples see the chaos happening all around them and fear for their lives. Meanwhile, Jesus is in the stern of the boat, "sleeping on a cushion" (Mark 4:38). He does not panic when they wake Him but simply gets up and rebukes the storm: "Quiet! Be still!" (verse 39). Immediately, the wind and the waves die down, leaving the disciples amazed that even the forces of nature obey Jesus.

In the second scene, the disciples are again out at sea. This time, Jesus isn't with them but watching from a mountainside. He sees them straining at the oars, "because the wind was against them" (6:48), and decides to come to their aid by walking on the waves. The disciples, from their vantage point, just see a shadowy figure about to pass them by and figure it is a ghost. So Jesus speaks to their fears, saying, "Take courage! It is I" (verse 50). He climbs into the boat, and immediately the wind dies down. His presence alone brings calm.

Jesus entered into the chaos to bring God's *shalom*. He calls you to bring God's peace to the storms in your world. When you are a peacemaker, you choose to step into broken systems, bruised relationships, and volatile rooms—not to control them but to reconcile them.

Meditate on God's Word: Genesis 1:1–5; Matthew 8:23–34; Romans 5:1–2

1. What currently represents chaos in your world? How do you think God might be calling you to step into that chaos to create peace?

2. Read Genesis 1:1–5. How is the earth described before God began His work of making it good? How did the Lord bring *shalom*—wholeness, harmony, peace—in creation?

Peace, in the biblical sense, is far more than a ceasefire or the mere absence of strife. The Hebrew word *shalom* conveys active wholeness, not passive calm. It is the comprehensive well-being of a person, society, or creation, rightly ordered under the reign of God. It's not just the end of conflict; it's the presence of harmony, justice, and delight. This peace restores the fractured world, not by sedating it, but by redeeming it. Biblical peace always touches four relational arenas: God, others, self, and creation.[37]

3. Read Matthew 8:23–34. This passage contains two stories of Jesus bringing peace. In the first, how did Jesus bring peace to the disciples when the storm arose at sea? What did the disciples recognize about Jesus' authority over chaos in this moment?

4. In the second story, how did Jesus bring peace to the demon-possessed man when He arrived in Gadarenes? What did the demons recognize about Jesus' authority over chaos in this moment?

Sin shattered all four relational arenas—God, others, self, and creation—leaving humanity alienated and disoriented. But in Christ, the great reconciliation begins. "Peace with God," Paul writes in Romans 5:1, becomes the foundation upon which all other peacemaking rests. The Puritan theologian Thomas Watson put it this way: "God the Son is called the Prince of Peace; He came into the world with a song of peace: 'on earth peace,' and He went out with a legacy of peace: 'My peace I give unto you.'"[38]

5. Read Romans 5:1–2. What enables you to have peace with God? Why is this the foundation upon which all other peacemaking is built?

ABIDE IN CHRIST

Pray that Jesus will give you the boldness to step into a conflict and the wisdom to know how to make peace in that particular situation. Thank Him for bringing His perfect peace that surpasses all understanding into your life. Check your schedule for today and plan at least two additional times to spend abiding in Christ.

Time #1: ______________________________

Time #2: ______________________________

STUDY 2

SPIRITUAL BATTLEGROUNDS

In contemporary warfare, the choice of battlefield is often driven by mission variables. Military commanders will identify terrain with natural barriers (like rivers and ridges) to set up strongpoints. They will also seek to secure the high ground to give them superior observation, better fields of fire, and defensive superiority. In the spiritual realm, it is likewise crucial to know the "terrain" of the battlefield and seek to secure the high ground.

Three areas in which the enemy tries to stir up chaos are the *home*, the *local church*, and the *world*. The home is a battleground because Satan knows that strong families raise strong followers of Jesus. So he seeks to weaken families in order to ruin the impact of future generations. The local church is a battleground because Satan knows the power a unified body of believers poses to his kingdom. So he tries to weaken the local church by creating divisions. The world is a battleground because it is where Satan naturally operates. If he can get believers to mirror the tone of the age, he can reduce their impact for the kingdom of God.

Peacemakers take the high ground in each area. In the home, they make Spirit-empowered choices to bless instead of blame, listen instead of react, and move toward each rather than turn away. In the church, they don't allow conflicts to divide them but confront sin gently, bear burdens generously, and stay engaged when it would be easier to walk away. In the world, they are not neutral but rooted. They recognize the struggle "is not against flesh and blood" (Ephesians 6:12) and refuse to turn people into enemies just because they disagree. In a world that fractures, they sow wholeness. They take up the armor of God daily so they are ready and prepared to fight the battle wherever it takes place.

Meditate on God's Word: Matthew 5:38–42; Ephesians 4:3–6; John 15:18–19

1. What are some of the ways you've seen the enemy stir up chaos in your home and local church? What affects you the most deeply about the chaos he stirs up in the world?

2. Read Matthew 5:38–42. What does Jesus say about taking the high ground when people provoke you? What does this imply about the cost involved in peacemaking?

> What makes peacemaking at home so costly is that it requires us to be both known and vulnerable. Family sees the worst of us. And yet, that is also what makes peace possible, because the gospel shines brightest where our sin is most exposed and still covered. Peacemaking is never clean. It means initiating awkward conversations when you'd rather shut down. It means giving the benefit of the doubt when you feel judged. It means putting the gospel to work where it matters most—not just in sermons or small groups but in apologies whispered in the kitchen or forgiveness offered through tears. Peace at home is forged through repentance, prayer, and long obedience in the same direction.[39]

3. Jesus said to His disciples, "Therefore I tell you, whatever you ask for in prayer, believe that you have received it, and it will be yours. And when you stand praying, if you hold anything against anyone, forgive them, so that your Father in heaven may forgive you your sins"(Mark 11:24–25). Jesus speaks not only about the power of prayer but also about the power of forgiveness. Who should be the first to forgive when a tense situation arises in the home? Why is it often so hard to be the one who takes that step?

In the church, peacemakers are essential to gospel witness. It's not the absence of conflict that marks a healthy church; it's the presence of people willing to confront sin gently, bear burdens generously, and stay at the table when it would be easier to walk away. Paul pleads in Ephesians 4:3 for believers to "Make every effort to keep the unity of the Spirit through the bond of peace." That phrase—"make every effort"—suggests intentionality, not passivity. Peace doesn't just happen in a congregation; it has to be pursued, protected, and practiced in the power of the Spirit.[40]

4. Read Ephesians 4:3–6. What appeal does the apostle Paul make for Christians to remain united? What part does peacemaking play in making that happen in the local church?

Out in the world, peacemakers stand out, not because they are passive but because they are principled. In a cultural moment defined by polarization, digital outrage, and tribal loyalty, peacemakers refuse to be discipled by the algorithm. They are not formed by TikTok feeds or news cycles but by the Word of God and the Spirit of Christ. Peacemakers don't just point out what's wrong; they live in a way that shows what could be right. And when they step into conflict, whether in civic life, social spaces, or neighborhood tensions, they carry not just opinions but the aroma of Christ.[41]

5. Read John 15:18–19. Why will you "stand out" in the world if you are following Jesus? How are you pointing out not just what is wrong in the world but what could be right?

ABIDE IN CHRIST

Pray for God's protection over your home and your local church. Ask that He would help you be an effective ambassador for His kingdom to a world clouded in darkness and in desperate need of a loving Savior. Check your schedule for today and plan at least two additional times when you will spend some focused time abiding in Christ.

Time #1: __________

Time #2: __________

STUDY 3

WILLING TO ACT

"All the believers were one in heart and mind. No one claimed that any of their possessions was their own, but they shared everything they had" (Acts 4:32). It's easy to read verses like these and romanticize what was taking place in the early church. Yes, there was unity, fellowship, and caring for one another. Yet, a short time later, we read there was also at least one dispute taking place: "The Hellenistic Jews among them complained against the Hebraic Jews because their widows were being overlooked in the daily distribution of food" (Acts 6:1).

Something had to be done to make peace. The feelings of the Hellenistic Jews couldn't be ignored, discounted, or dismissed. The Twelve (the disciples of Jesus) had to step up as peacemakers so that bitterness would not take root in the church. They seem to have recognized that spiritual and material concerns are so closely related that one always impacts the other—for better or for worse. They did not assign blame to either party or side with one group over the other.[42] They simply called everyone together to devise a solution.

The idea the Twelve came up with was for the church to appoint seven men to oversee the proper distribution of food while they focused on "prayer and the ministry of the word" (verse 4). The result? "This proposal pleased the whole group" (verse 5). The crisis was averted . . . but only because the Twelve were willing to take action.

In the church today, it's easy to mistake the absence of tension for the presence of peace. However, avoiding difficult conversations isn't *peacemaking*; it's *passivity*. Peacemakers don't avoid tension but step into it. They rely on Jesus and enter into the mess, knowing they are being held by the One who has already secured the ultimate peace.

Meditate on God's Word: Romans 12:17–18; 1 Corinthians 1:10–17; Acts 6:1–7

1. What are some of the biggest obstacles for you when it comes to making peace? What have you learned this week that can help you overcome some of those hurdles?

2. Read Romans 12:17–18. What does Paul say you *shouldn't* do if you want to make peace? What does Paul say you *should* actively do to create peace?

A major obstacle to peacemaking is the slow corrosion of bitterness. Hebrews 12:15 warns us to see to it that "no root of bitterness springs up, causing trouble and defiling many" (CSB). That's the danger: Bitterness never stays contained. It spills out in sarcasm, avoidance, passive aggression, and subtle withdrawal. Bitterness is pain that has hardened into pride. It refuses to release the offender, hoping that harboring anger will somehow even the scales. But here's the irony: While we wait for the other person to suffer, we end up poisoning our own souls.[43]

---

3. Read 1 Corinthians 1:10–17. How did Paul act as a peacemaker in this passage? What appeal did he make to the church to bring them back together?

4. Read Acts 6:1–7. Before Jesus, the Jews and Gentiles (Hellenists) had led separate lives, but now they were joined into one body. How might their former cultural/religious separation have played a role in sparking this conflict?

Perhaps the most subtle and culturally reinforced obstacle to peacemaking is the idolatry of comfort. Comfort is a powerful force. We avoid hard conversations not because we don't care but because we want to stay undisturbed. We tell ourselves, *It's not worth it* or *I'll let it go*, when what we really mean is, *I don't want to feel awkward, tired, stretched, or misunderstood*. But the gospel is not built on comfort. It's built on a cross. And if Jesus moved toward us while we were still enemies (Romans 5:8), how can we settle for peace that requires no movement at all?[44]

5. Why was it important for the Twelve (the disciples of Jesus) to not allow any desire "to stay undisturbed" affect their decision to intervene? What do you learn from their example of how to *effectively* be a peacemaker so that both sides feel heard and respected?

ABIDE IN CHRIST

Pray that Jesus would give you His peace and help you in your ongoing efforts to be His peacemaker. Check your schedule for today and plan at least two additional times when you will spend some focused time abiding in Christ and praying for peace.

Time #1: ____________________

Time #2: ____________________

JOIN IN COMMUNITY

Connect with another Christ-follower this week to discuss some of the key insights from this session. Use any of the following prompts to help guide your discussion.

- What did you learn this week about being a peacemaker that especially caught your attention? Why did that stand out to you?
- What part does knowing who you are in Christ play when it comes to not engaging in unhealthy comparison or competition with others?
- What currently represents chaos in your world? How have you been able to step into that chaos this week to create peace?
- What is hardest for you about taking the "high ground" when people purposefully seek to provoke you?
- What are some of the major obstacles you confront when it comes to making peace? How has God been helping you to overcome those hurdles?

Use this time to go back and complete any of the study and reflection questions from previous days that you weren't able to finish. Make a note below of any revelations you've had and reflect on any growth or personal insights you've gained.

Read chapters 10–11 in *Becoming Like Jesus*. Use the space below to make note of anything in those chapters that stands out to you or encourages you.

WEEK 6 *at a glance*

THIS WEEK'S READING	Chapters 10–11 in *Becoming Like Jesus*
GROUP MEETING	Read the Welcome and Connect with the group (page 112) Watch the video and take notes (pages 113–114) Discuss the questions that follow (page 115) Respond to the teaching and Close (page 116)
PERSONAL STUDIES: STUDY 1 STUDY 2 STUDY 3	 "Visible Targets" (pages 119–122) "A Deeper Cut" (pages 123–126) "Stay in the Race" (pages 127–130)
WRAP UP THE STUDY	Connect with someone in your group during the week Complete any unfinished studies (page 131)

SESSION SIX

PERSECUTED AND REJOICING: THE COST AND CROWN

"Blessed are those who are persecuted because of righteousness, for theirs is the kingdom of heaven. Blessed are you when people insult you, persecute you and falsely say all kinds of evil against you because of me. Rejoice and be glad, because great is your reward in heaven, for in the same way they persecuted the prophets who were before you."

MATTHEW 5:10-12

WELCOME | READ ON YOUR OWN

As you have seen throughout this study, the Beatitudes kind of "dance" with each other. You enter into the horizontal coil of the spiritual life with poverty of spirit and grief over sin. You take that humility into your relationships and commit to seeking after righteousness. The truth you discover about God's mercy compels you to lead a pure life and show mercy to others. You then bring the peace of God into all your interactions with people.

This leads to what you could call the culmination of the Beatitudes. Jesus has been establishing what it looks like to be His follower, but He wants to be up-front in saying there will be times when things will get difficult, painful, and dangerous. The promise is that you will be blessed when you are *persecuted* because of righteousness. Getting even more specific (and personal), Jesus adds that this blessing extends to when people also insult you and speak all kinds of evil against you—something that certainly was happening to Him and His disciples.

Persecution looks different today in different parts of the world. Yet all persecution, in whatever form or degree it occurs, is painful, unsettling, and disturbing. And the promise is the same. You can rejoice and be glad, because great is your reward in heaven when you suffer for righteousness. This is the great hope that serves as an anchor in the storm.

CONNECT | 10 MINUTES

Get this session started by discussing one of these questions:

- What is something that spoke to you in last week's personal study that you would like to share with the group?

  — or —

- In what ways have you experienced being insulted, spoken falsely about, or even persecuted because of your faith in Jesus?

WATCH | 25 MINUTES

Now watch the video for this session. Below is an outline of the key points covered during the teaching. Record any key concepts that stand out to you.

OUTLINE

I. Persecution is part of the journey in becoming more like Jesus.

A. Jesus said you will be persecuted simply for living your life in a righteous manner.

B. People may come after you for refusing to use your gifts for unrighteousness.

C. You may be persecuted because you work to bring order, beauty, and goodness.

II. Persecution reveals the conflict occurring between God's kingdom and the world.

A. The kingdom of God and the kingdom of the world are in constant opposition.

B. You are called to push back the darkness and establish the light of Christ wherever you are.

C. Awareness of this spiritual conflict will steady your soul and help you endure persecution with courage.

III. Engage in the deep work of becoming like Christ to endure persecution.

A. You need to be anchored in the Word of God and bring your honest prayers to Him.

B. Endurance develops over time through small trials that prepare you for greater challenges to come.

C. God will use persecution to strengthen your faith and produce lasting spiritual fruit in your life.

IV. Your community of believers is essential for standing firm in persecution.

A. Belonging to a local church provides support, encouragement, and accountability.

B. Isolation makes you vulnerable to attacks, while community offers refuge and strength.

C. The kingdom of God belongs to all followers of Christ even as they are being persecuted.

NOTES

DISCUSS | 35 MINUTES

Discuss what you just watched by answering the following questions.

1. Ask someone in the group to read aloud Matthew 5:10–12. What *general* statement does Jesus make about those who are persecuted for righteousness? What *personal* comment does He then make for the benefit of His followers?

2. Jesus said that He had come "to bring fire on the earth" and that people (even families) "will be divided" because of the gospel (Luke 12:49, 53). What does this say about the nature of being a Christ-follower? What kind of division does it naturally bring?

3. Ask someone to read aloud 1 Peter 4:1–5. What link does Peter make between persecution and refusing to live as the world lives? When have you suffered persecution not because of what you *did* but because of what you *wouldn't* do?

4. Paul wrote, "Have nothing to do with the fruitless deeds of darkness, but rather expose them" (Ephesians 5:11). What does it look like to expose the deeds of darkness in our culture today? When has God asked you to actually step up and do this?

5. Ask someone to read aloud 2 Corinthians 10:3–6. It is important to recognize that persecution comes because you are in a spiritual battle. What does Paul say about the war you fight? What are the "weapons" you've been given to wage this battle?

RESPOND | 10 MINUTES

Shallow-rooted Christianity will not hold up when *persecution* comes. It takes the deep work of developing endurance to weather trials and grow through them—and the only way endurance comes is by enduring. As Paul writes, you have to be intentional about building up your endurance:

> 25 Everyone who competes in the games goes into strict training. They do
> it to get a crown that will not last, but we do it to get a crown that will
> last forever. 26 Therefore I do not run like someone running aimlessly; I do
> not fight like a boxer beating the air. 27 No, I strike a blow to my body and
> make it my slave so that after I have preached to others, I myself will not
> be disqualified for the prize.
>
> **1 CORINTHIANS 9:25-27**

In what way is developing spiritual endurance like training for a competition? What kind of "strict training" do you find is required to develop spiritual endurance?

What does Paul say your focus should be as you train your heart and mind? How could keeping this aim in mind help you weather the storms of persecution?

CLOSE | 10 MINUTES

Close your time in this study by thanking Jesus for revealing what it means to grow in your faith and become like Him. Praise Him for the journey and for the Holy Spirit to continue to develop your spiritual endurance so you can stand up for righteousness whatever comes your way. Also pray for the believers all around the world who are experiencing the life-and-death reality of being persecuted for their faith. Pray that God would give them His strength to endure.

SESSION SIX

PERSONAL STUDY

You're probably not a fan of how Jesus ended the list of Beatitudes. Are you really supposed to consider yourself happy and blessed when you are *persecuted* for living a life of righteousness? Why not end on a more positive note? In fact, Jesus does end the Beatitudes with an encouraging word, because you—His follower—know there is more to your existence than this life. Yes, you will experience the blessings of God's kingdom in the here and now, but you are also promised an eternal reward for your faithfulness to Christ. Keep this in mind as you work through these exercises, and stay engaged in your community! Continue to share in the weeks and months ahead what you are learning. If you have been reading *Becoming Like Jesus* alongside this study, you may want to first review chapters 10–11 of the book.

"Love your enemies and pray for those who persecute you."

MATTHEW 5:44

STUDY 1

VISIBLE TARGETS

On September 1, 1939, regulations for blackouts were imposed in Britain. These rules required all windows and doors to be covered at night and all external lights to be switched off or dimmed. The reason? The country was preparing for war with Germany, and the lights made it easy for enemy bombers to locate and attack the British cities.

Jesus told His followers, "You are the light of the world. A town built on a hill cannot be hidden" (Matthew 5:14). You are called to be a visible representation of God's divine light in a world filled with spiritual darkness. You are to be a light that everyone—including the enemy of your soul—can clearly see. In this way, you follow after Jesus, who is "the light of the world" (John 9:5). You live your life, as Paul proclaimed, "as children of light" (Ephesians 5:8).

Satan, of course, wants to extinguish your light. This means that you, as a light-bearer, will be under constant attack. And unlike the British citizens in World War II, you can't cover up or switch off your light when you feel an enemy bomber is approaching. Jesus said, "If they persecuted me, they will persecute you also" (John 15:20). Paul likewise wrote, "Everyone who wants to live a godly life in Christ Jesus will be persecuted" (2 Timothy 3:12). Persecution comes in different shapes and forms, but the fundamental truth is that it *does* come.

Still, Jesus tells you, "Rejoice and be glad, for your reward is great in heaven" (Matthew 5:12 ESV). When Jesus says this, it doesn't mean He is glorifying the pain you will endure as His light-bearer. Rather, He is giving you a new lens through which to interpret the suffering you will experience. When you are mocked, misrepresented, or mistreated for His name, you are being drawn into His story. You are moving through the coil of becoming like Jesus.

Meditate on God's Word: Matthew 5:14–16; 2 Corinthians 2:14–17; 1 Peter 4:15–16

1. What are some of the ways the enemy has recently attacked you or your family? What unsettles you the most when you experience one of these attacks?

2. Read Matthew 5:14–16. What is Jesus' instruction to you as His disciple? What is the ultimate goal of allowing your "light" to shine before others?

> As we become like Jesus, we begin to live differently, we pursue holiness, and we hunger for righteousness. This is deeply convicting to those who have given themselves over to the loves of this world. It disorients and maybe even angers them. Persecution bubbles up from here. Jesus wants us to know that it's coming, to expect it. In doing so, He prepares us not only for the pain of resistance but for the reward of resilience.[45]

3. Read 2 Corinthians 2:14–17. How does Paul describe the way that God had led him? What had the Lord enabled Paul to spread everywhere he went?

4. What "aroma" did Paul and his coworkers bring to those who had given themselves over to the loves of this world? How had Paul presented the gospel of Christ to all?

Not all suffering is blessed. There's no blessing in being obnoxious in the name of Jesus. There's no crown for belligerence, for stirring up drama over minor theological squabbles, or for wielding truth like a weapon instead of a balm. Don't confuse persecution with consequences for unchristian behavior. What Jesus blesses is the suffering that comes from living in such a way that the aroma of Christ clings to you.[46]

5. Read 1 Peter 4:15–16. What kind of suffering is *not* blessed? How do you know when your suffering is truly coming as a result of your testimony for Jesus?

ABIDE IN CHRIST

Pray that you will continue to serve as a shining light for God's kingdom. Ask Jesus to give you a new lens through which to interpret the suffering you endure for His sake. Review your schedule for today and plan at least two additional times to check in with Him.

Time #1: ______________________

Time #2: ______________________

STUDY 2

A DEEPER CUT

Persecution usually brings to mind the violent ending of a saint's life. Figures like the disciple James, who was beheaded by King Herod Agrippa. Or Stephen, a deacon in the early church who was put to death by the Jewish leaders. Or later figures in the church like Polycarp, a disciple of John, who was burned at the stake for refusing to recant his faith.

The persecution you face for Christ likely won't be this overt. In most cases, it will take the form of words directed toward you—or words spoken behind your back—that will deeply pierce your heart. It might also take the form of subtle actions taken by others in your life to discredit you, dismiss you, or disregard you. You might be ostracized by coworkers because you won't compromise your integrity. You might be chastised on social media because you don't hold to the majority view. You might not receive an invitation to certain gatherings that others in the neighborhood are attending because of your Christian beliefs.

It's one thing when persecution comes from people in the world. The hope is that after everything they've put you through, the aroma of Jesus will become irresistible to them and they will put their faith in Him. But it's a much deeper cut when the persecution comes from a fellow brother or sister in Christ. You can be shocked (and disoriented) by how cruel other Christians can be. But even in this, you can follow the example of Jesus.

During His time on earth, Jesus was called a glutton, a drunkard, and a sinner by the very people He came to save. The Jewish religious leaders plotted against Him and, ultimately, condemned Him on false testimony. Jesus knows what it is like to be wounded by those who should be supporting you. He will meet you in the midst of that persecution.

Meditate on God's Word: Proverbs 10:9; 11:3; Psalm 41:1–13; John 13:21–30

1. What are some of the criticisms you have received in your life because you chose to follow after Jesus? How have you handled those attacks against you?

2. Read Proverbs 10:9 and 11:3. You know the *cost* of living with integrity, but what is the *reward*? What do these proverbs say will happen to those who take crooked paths?

Persecution doesn't always come with jail time or broken bones. Sometimes, it arrives as a whisper. It's the slow burn of slander, the ache of being misunderstood, the sting of false accusations from people who should know better. That's why Jesus turns in Matthew 5:11 and speaks directly to His disciples—not in the abstract but in the personal: "Blessed are you when others revile you, persecute you and utter all kinds of evil against you falsely on my account" (ESV). He moves from saying "blessed are those" in the Beatitude to "you" in this following verse—from a general description to an intimate address—because this kind of persecution doesn't just bruise the body; it is deeply intimate and wounds the heart. To be misrepresented by strangers is hard. To be misrepresented by brothers and sisters in Christ can be devastating.[47]

3. Read David's honest prayer to God in Psalm 41:1–8. What words are David's enemies speaking against him? What "whispers" is he hearing from them?

4. Continue reading Psalm 41:9–13. What does David say in this section about his close friend? Where does David find strength and assurance in the midst of all these attacks?

There is something especially painful about being misunderstood when your motives are sincere. Jesus was no stranger to this pain. He was accused of being demon-possessed, plotted against by religious leaders, abandoned by friends, and ultimately condemned on false testimony. Isaiah called Him "a man of sorrows, and acquainted with grief" (Isaiah 53:3 ESV). He knows what it is to be falsely accused and deeply wounded by those He came to love. That's why He meets us in our reviling, not with distant sympathy but with divine solidarity.[48]

5. Read John 13:21–30. Jesus knows what it is like to be betrayed by a friend. How does it help you to know that He can identify with this kind of pain?

ABIDE IN CHRIST

Pray for patience in your dealings with your fellow believers in Christ. Commit to forgive others as Jesus has forgiven you. Honestly express your feelings to the Lord about any betrayals you have suffered in the past. Review your schedule for today and write down at least two additional times to spend time with Jesus and abide in Him.

Time #1: ______________________

Time #2: ______________________

STUDY 3

STAY IN THE RACE

The journey of becoming like Jesus isn't a solo sprint . . . or even a marathon. It's more like adventure racing. If you haven't heard of the sport, it's a navigation-based event where teams use maps and compasses to traverse wilderness courses. It combines trekking, mountain biking, paddling, climbing, and problem-solving, with team members working together to adjust strategies and overcome challenges. Races can last for days or even weeks.

As you move through the sideways coil that is the spiritual life, your progress will be marked by repetition and struggle. You will have to do the deep work, over time, of repeatedly looping through the Beatitudes as God adjusts your course and steadily moves you forward. But don't forget the process is also marked by *grace*. God has promised, "Never will I leave you; never will I forsake you" (Hebrews 13:5). So you can say with confidence, "The Lord is my helper; I will not be afraid. What can mere mortals do to me?" (verse 6).

Also remember that unlike a solo event, you have teammates in the race you are running. You have brothers and sisters in Christ who, like you, are seeking to become Beatitude people. It's easy to think the Holy Spirit only works through quiet times and spiritual disciplines, but the reality is that He also works through human interactions. He will use your community to test and train you. Every relational bump in the trail is like a chisel in God's hands. Often, it is the people closest to you who reveal your deepest wounds and need for grace.

The challenge, as you come to the end of this study, is to *keep going*. Stay engaged in the "adventure race" you are running. Keep your eyes fixed on the prize. And treat every hilltop and valley as part of the same coil the Holy Spirit is using to shape you into the image of Christ.

Meditate on God's Word: 2 Corinthians 12:1–10; 2 Timothy 4:1–8; Galatians 6:9–10

1. What has encouraged you the most over the course of this study as you have done the deep work of becoming more like Jesus? What progress have you seen toward becoming a Beatitude person—and how has your community helped in this growth?

2. Read 2 Corinthians 12:1–10. How does Paul describe his spiritual journey? What had he learned about God's grace in the midst of his weaknesses?

> Sanctification is not a sprint; it is the slow-burning perseverance of grace in motion. It takes time, real time. Not the thirty-day-plan kind, or the "read a book and fix it" kind. The Spirit works in seasons, not seconds. We live in a culture obsessed with shortcuts, but holiness has never had one. I know a woman who came to faith at age twenty, and now in her seventies, even though she still wrestles with envy, she can name it more quickly, surrender it faster, and trust Jesus more deeply. That's not regression; that's formation. You're not supposed to be done. You're supposed to be being made. When we embrace that the journey is long, we stop judging ourselves by today's failures and start trusting in God's faithfulness over decades. This is the long arc of obedience.[49]

3. Read 2 Timothy 4:1–8. What did Paul charge Timothy to do "in season and out of season"—in other words, over the course of his life?

4. How did Paul describe the race that he had been running? What was his focus and priority now that his race was coming to an end?

> Formation isn't neutral. You're either being shaped more into Christ's image or into something else. That's why perseverance matters so deeply. Sanctification isn't a lightning strike. It's a long obedience, a slow burn, a daily decision to stay in the story God is telling through your life. The enemy doesn't have to destroy you if he can just distract you or convince you to quit. But grace gives you the courage to stay.[50]

5. Read Galatians 6:9–10. How do these words encourage you to *keep going* in the good work that you have been doing of becoming more like Jesus?

ABIDE IN CHRIST

Spend some extended time today praising God for never leaving you, for His gift of grace, and for leading you through the horizontal coil of the spiritual life. Pray that you ever-increasingly become more like Jesus. Look at your schedule one last time and write down at least two additional times when you will check in with Jesus today.

Time #1: ______________________________

Time #2: ______________________________

WRAP UP THE STUDY

Connect with another Christ-follower this week to discuss some of the key insights from this session. Use any of the following prompts to help guide your discussion.

- Jesus said that people "will be divided" because of the gospel (Luke 12:53). What does this say about the nature of being a Christ-follower?
- What does it look like to expose the deeds of darkness in your culture? When has God asked you to step up and do this?
- What are some of the ways the enemy has recently attacked you or your family? What is most unsettling when you experience these attacks?
- Jesus knows what it is like to be betrayed by a friend. How does it help you to know that He can identify with this kind of pain?
- What progress have you seen over the course of this study in becoming a Beatitude person? How has your community helped in this growth?

Use this time to go back and complete any of the study and reflection questions from previous days that you weren't able to finish. Make note of what God has revealed to you in these days. Finally, talk with your group about which study you may want to go through next. Put a date on the calendar for when you'll meet next to study God's Word and dive deeper into community.

LEADER'S GUIDE

Thank you for your willingness to lead your group! What you are doing is valuable and will make a difference in the lives of others. *Becoming Like Jesus* is a six-session Bible study built around video content and small-group interaction. As the group leader, imagine yourself as the host of a party. Your job is to take care of your guests by managing the details so that when your guests arrive, they can focus on one another and on the interaction around the topic for that session.

Your role as the group leader is not to answer all the questions or reteach the content—the video, book, and study guide will do most of that work. Your job is to guide the experience and cultivate your small group into a connected and engaged community. This will make it a place for members to process, question, and reflect—not necessarily to receive more instruction. There are several elements in this leader's guide that will help you as you structure your study and reflection time, so be sure to follow along and take advantage of each one.

BEFORE YOU BEGIN

Before your first meeting, make sure the group members have a copy of this study guide. Alternately, you can hand out the study guides at your first meeting and give the members some time to look over the material and ask any preliminary questions. Also, make sure the group members are aware they have access to the streaming videos at any time by following the instructions provided with this guide. During your first meeting, ask the members to provide their names, phone numbers, and email addresses so that you can keep in touch.

Generally, the ideal size for a group is eight to ten people, which will ensure that everyone has enough time to participate in discussions. If you have more people, break up the main group into smaller subgroups. Encourage those who show up at the first meeting to commit to attending for the duration of the study, as this will help the group members get to know one another, create stability for the group, and help you know how best to prepare to lead the participants through the material.

Each session begins with an opening reflection in the Welcome section. The questions that follow in the Connect section serve as icebreakers to get the group members thinking about the topic. In the rest of the study, it's generally not a good idea to have everyone answer every question—a free-flowing discussion is more desirable. But with the icebreaker question, you can go around the circle and ask each person to respond. Encourage shy people to share, but don't force them.

At your first meeting, let the group members know each session also contains a personal study section they can use to continue to engage with the content until the next meeting. While doing this section is optional, it will help them cement the concepts presented during the group study time and help them better understand how to adopt Jesus' teachings in the Beatitudes.

Let them know that, if they choose to do so, they can watch the video for the next session by accessing the streaming code provided with this study guide. Invite them to bring any questions and insights to your next meeting, especially if they had a breakthrough moment or didn't understand something.

PREPARATION FOR EACH SESSION

As the leader of your group, there are a few things you should do to best prepare for each meeting:

- **Read through the session.** This will help you become more familiar with the content and know how to structure the discussion times.
- **Decide how the videos will be used.** Determine whether you want the members to watch the videos ahead of time (again, via the streaming access code provided with this study guide) or together as a group.
- **Decide which questions you want to discuss.** Based on the length of your group discussions, you may not be able to get through all the questions. So look over the discussion questions provided in each session and mark which ones you definitely want to cover.

- **Be familiar with the questions you want to discuss.** When the group meets, you'll be watching the clock, so make sure you are familiar with the questions you have selected.
- **Pray for your group.** Pray for your group members and ask God to lead them as they study His Word and listen to His Spirit.

In many cases, there will be no one "right" answer to the questions. Answers will vary, especially when the group members are sharing their personal experiences.

STRUCTURING THE DISCUSSION TIME

You will need to determine with your group how long you want your meetings to last so that you can plan your time accordingly. Suggested times for each section have been provided in this study guide, and if you adhere to these times, your group will meet for ninety minutes. However, many groups like to meet for two hours. If this describes your particular group, follow the times listed in the right-hand column of the chart given below.

Section	90 Minutes	120 Minutes
CONNECT (discuss one or more of the opening questions for the session)	10 minutes	15 minutes
WATCH (watch the teaching material together and take notes)	25 minutes	25 minutes
DISCUSS (discuss the study questions you selected ahead of time)	35 minutes	50 minutes
RESPOND (write down takeaways)	10 minutes	15 minutes
CLOSE (pray together and dismiss)	10 minutes	15 minutes

As the group leader, it is up to you to keep track of the time and to keep things on schedule. You might want to set a timer for each segment so that both you and the group members know when the time is up. (There are some good phone apps for timers that play a gentle chime or other pleasant sound instead of a disruptive noise.)

Don't be concerned if group members are quiet or slow to share. People are often quiet when they are pulling together their ideas, and this might be a new experience for some of them. Just ask a question and let it hang in the air until someone shares. You can then say, "Thank you. What about others? What came to you when you watched that portion of the teaching?"

GROUP DYNAMICS

Leading a group through *Becoming Like Jesus* will prove to be highly rewarding both to you and your group members. But you still may encounter challenges along the way! Discussions can get off track. Group members may not be sensitive to the needs and ideas of others. Some might worry that they will be expected to talk about matters that make them feel awkward. Others may express comments that result in disagreements.

To help ease this strain on you and the group, consider the following ground rules:

- When someone raises a question or comment that is off the main topic, suggest you deal with it another time, or, if you feel led to go in that direction, tell the group you will be spending some time discussing it.

- If someone asks a question that you don't know how to answer, admit it and move on. At your discretion, feel free to invite group members to comment on questions that call for personal experience.

- If you find that one or two people are dominating the discussion time, direct a few questions to others in the group. Outside the main group time, ask the more dominating members to help you draw out the quieter ones. Work to make them part of the solution instead of part of the problem.

- When a disagreement occurs, encourage the group members to process the matter in love. Encourage those on opposite sides to restate what they heard the other side say about the matter, and then invite each side to evaluate if that perception is accurate. Lead the group in examining other passages related to the topic and look for common ground.

When any of these issues arise, encourage your group members to follow these words from Scripture: "Love one another" (John 13:34); "If it is possible, as far as it depends on you, live at peace with everyone" (Romans 12:18); "Whatever is true . . . noble . . . right . . . pure . . . lovely . . . if anything is excellent or praiseworthy—think about such things" (Philippians 4:8); and, "Everyone should be quick to listen, slow to speak and slow to become angry" (James 1:19). This will make your group time more rewarding and beneficial for everyone who attends.

Thank you for taking the time to lead your group. You are making a difference in your members' lives and having an impact on their journey toward a better understanding of what it means to move along the horizontal coil of becoming like Jesus.

NOTES

1. Charles Haddon Spurgeon, "The Sixth Beatitude," sermon no. 3159, delivered April 27, 1873, https://www.spurgeon.org/resource-library/sermons/the-sixth-beatitude/#flipbook/.
2. Matt Chandler, *Becoming Like Jesus: The Everyday Journey to Living a Life of Holiness* (W Publishing, 2026), 6.
3. Chandler, *Becoming Like Jesus*, 7.
4. Chandler, *Becoming Like Jesus*, 8–9.
5. Chandler, *Becoming Like Jesus*, 11.
6. Chandler, *Becoming Like Jesus*, 20.
7. Chandler, *Becoming Like Jesus*, 21.
8. Chandler, *Becoming Like Jesus*, 30.
9. Donald A. Carson, "Matthew," *The Expositor's Bible Commentary*, vol. 9 (Zondervan Academic, 2010) 404–405.
10. Chandler, *Becoming Like Jesus*, 31–32. Quote from John Chrysostom taken from Philip Schaff, "The Greek and Latin Creeds," *The Creeds of Christendom*, vol. 2 (Harper & Brothers, 1890), 514.
11. Allen C. Myers, "Kingdom," *The Eerdmans Bible Dictionary* (Eerdmans, 1987), 625.
12. Stephen Um, *The Kingdom of God*, The Gospel Coalition (Crossway, 2011), 10.
13. Chandler, *Becoming Like Jesus*, 41.
14. Oswald Chambers, "Repentance," *My Utmost for His Highest: Selections for the Year*, December 7 (Oswald Chambers Publications; Marshall Pickering, 1986).
15. Chandler, *Becoming Like Jesus*, 37.
16. Chandler, *Becoming Like Jesus*, 46.
17. Chandler, *Becoming Like Jesus*, 51.
18. Chandler, *Becoming Like Jesus*, 58.
19. The King James Version translates the Hebrew *anav* and Greek *praus* as "meek": "Now the man Moses was very meek [*anav*], above all the men which were upon the face of the earth" (Numbers 12:3); "Take my yoke upon you, and learn of me; for I am meek [*praus*] and lowly in heart: and ye shall find rest unto your souls" (Matthew 11:29).
20. Chandler, *Becoming Like Jesus*, 78–79.
21. Chandler, *Becoming Like Jesus*, 82–83.
22. Jean Anthelme Brillat-Savarin, *The Physiology of Taste*, aphorism IV.
23. Stav Dimitropoulos, "You Really Are What You Eat, Science Says," Olive Oil Times, January 10, 2017, https://www.oliveoiltimes.com/health-news/really-eat-science-says/54739.
24. Chandler, *Becoming Like Jesus*, 88–89.
25. Chandler, *Becoming Like Jesus*, 95.
26. Chandler, *Becoming Like Jesus*, 96.
27. Chandler, *Becoming Like Jesus*, 100–101.
28. Chandler, *Becoming Like Jesus*, 105.
29. Chandler, *Becoming Like Jesus*, 111.

30. Walter L. Liefeld and David W. Pao, "Luke," *The Expositor's Bible Commentary*, vol. 10 (Zondervan Academic, 2007), 125.
31. Chandler, *Becoming Like Jesus*, 116.
32. Chandler, *Becoming Like Jesus*, 126.
33. Chandler, *Becoming Like Jesus*, 129.
34. Guidelines for how much mustard could be planted alongside other crops were even developed in the third century AD. According to the Mishnah, Kil'ayim 2:9, "If there were one or two patches [in a field of grain], he sows them with mustard; [but if there were] three [patches], he shalt not sow them [with] mustard, for [then the field as a whole] looks like a field of mustard," the words of R. Meir. And the sages say, "Nine patches are permitted, [but] ten are prohibited [it is permitted to lay out no more than nine patches of mustard in a field of grain.]"
35. Chandler, *Becoming Like Jesus*, 118.
36. Chandler, *Becoming Like Jesus*, 138.
37. Chandler, *Becoming Like Jesus*, 145.
38. Chandler, *Becoming Like Jesus*, 145. Quote from Thomas Watson taken from Thomas Watson, *The Beatitudes: An Exposition of Matthew 5:1–12* (Banner of Truth, 1971), 276.
39. Chandler, *Becoming Like Jesus*, 151.
40. Chandler, *Becoming Like Jesus*, 151.
41. Chandler, *Becoming Like Jesus*, 153.
42. Richard N. Longenecker, "Acts," *The Expositor's Bible Commentary*, vol. 10 (Zondervan Academic, 2007), 805.
43. Chandler, *Becoming Like Jesus*, 156.
44. Chandler, *Becoming Like Jesus*, 157.
45. Chandler, *Becoming Like Jesus*, 164.
46. Chandler, *Becoming Like Jesus*, 165.
47. Chandler, *Becoming Like Jesus*, 172–173.
48. Chandler, *Becoming Like Jesus*, 173–174.
49. Chandler, *Becoming Like Jesus*, 193.
50. Chandler, *Becoming Like Jesus*, 207.

ABOUT MATT CHANDLER

Matt Chandler is a husband, father, pastor, elder, and author whose greatest desire is to make much of Jesus. He has served for over twenty years as the Lead Pastor at The Village Church in Flower Mound, Texas, which recently transitioned its five campuses into their own autonomous churches. He is also the Executive Chairman of the Acts 29 Network, a large church-planting community that trains and equips church planters across the globe. Matt is known around the world for proclaiming the gospel in a powerful and down-to-earth way and enjoys traveling to share the message of Jesus whenever he can. He lives in Texas with his beautiful wife, Lauren, and their three children: Audrey, Reid, and Norah.

From the Publisher

GREAT STUDIES

ARE EVEN BETTER WHEN THEY'RE SHARED!

Help others find this study:

- Post a review at your favorite online bookseller.
- Post a picture on a social media account and share why you enjoyed it.
- Send a note to a friend who would also love it—or, better yet, go through it with them!

Thanks for helping others grow their faith!

www.ingramcontent.com/pod-product-compliance
Lightning Source LLC
LaVergne TN
LVHW031120060826
845145LV00014B/3028
9780310165279